THE DEEPER THINGS

BLIND FAITH II

BRITTANY LENORE

THE DEEPER THINGS

All scripture quotations, citing, or otherwise indicated are taken from the NASB (New American Standard Bible®, Copyright© 1960, 1962, 1963, 1968, 1971, 1972, 1973, 1975, 1977, 1995 by The Lockman Foundation); NKJV (The Holy Bible, New King James Version, Copyright © 1982 Nashville. Thomas Nelson); American Standard Version, Copyright © 1995; original work published 1971, Thomas Nelson; The Holy Bible, New International Version, NIV® Copyright © 1973, 1978, 1984, 2011 by Biblica, Inc.®); The Holy Bible, English Standard Version® (ESV®) Copyright © 2001 by Crossway; The Holy Bible, NLT (New Living Translations, Copyright © 2015 by Tindale House Publishers); KJV (King James Version, used under public domain).

Some details in stories or recollections have been changed to protect the identities of the people or locations involved.

ISBN: 978-1-7355144-4-4

978-1-7355144-1-3 (paperback)
978-1-7355144-3-7 (ebook)

Copyright © 2021 by Brittany Lenore Moore

Cover Concept by Brittany Lenore Moore
Photography by Jason Thomas | JL Photography
www.jlasan.com
Formatting, Design & Editing by Chadash LLC,
www.chadashdesign.com

All rights reserved. No part of this book may be reproduced or transmitted in any form or by any means, electronic or mechanical, including photocopying and recording, or by any information storage and retrieval system, without the express written permission by the author or publisher.

Published and Printed in the United States of America. 2021
– First Edition

Availability For Sale

BE SURE TO PURCHASE *"BLIND FAITH"* on **www.amazon.com**. This book follows up on a few incidents that occurred in the original "*Blind Faith*" book.

DEDICATION

To My Supporters:

I dedicate this book to you. I have learned that as life happens, by walking in pure faith, God always sends you the right people at the right time. Those people that I am referring to are you, whether that comes in the form of a DM, sharing something I posted on social media, sending me text messages or voice notes of how proud you are of me, calling me on the phone and making me laugh, encouraging me to keep going, reminding me that my journey is not in vain and that people are being touched by my ministry, they're PRAYING for me and even releasing the Word of the Lord over my life at just the right time. I truly want to say thanks to all of you who make my journey worth it.

I want to encourage you all to move by the Spirit of God at any cost. Truly begin to study the *DEEPER THINGS OF GOD* by reading His Word and studying the scriptures. God's Word is life, and it is something that will forever keep us drawn to who He is in our lives no matter what. He is our Father. And no matter who abandons us or rejects us, He will NEVER abandon or reject us. Don't listen to people who say prayer doesn't work. They honestly haven't gone deep enough in the presence of God and the highest of the Heavens to see mountains (hardships, mental attacks, illnesses) moved in their lives. Take it from me, from a woman who weeps on her face day in and day out, a woman who wars not only for herself but on behalf of others constantly, a woman who teaches others the importance of prayer and a woman who relies on prayer to get her through each day, prayer works.

And to each person: Your prayer life is your weapon to every natural problem in your life. I charge you, as a believer of JESUS CHRIST, to ask GOD to take you deeper by showing you great and mighty things of the Kingdom of God through the power of the Holy Spirit. What awaits you is far greater than anything you will see with your natural eyes. I love each and every one of you so much! To the ones I know personally, to the ones that I don't know and hope to meet in the future, God does not make mistakes. Whatever it is, give it to Him and trust Him wholeheartedly this next season of your life. Remember, if you've survived through the 2020 Coronavirus Pandemic, then you can survive any other storm roaring in your life with the help of our Lord and Savior. God is greater than the highs and the lows.

The Deeper Things of journeying through *Blind Faith II* will cause you to adjust your prayer life.

Brittany Lenore

CONTENTS

Ch. 1 | Flewed (Flown) Out to NYC 1

Ch. 2 | Misshapes & Miracles 14

Ch. 3 | Location, Location, Location 19

Ch. 4 | Home For The Holidays 38
            Watch Party Night...............................41

Ch. 5 | Switching Lanes 45
            He Is Still In The Picture: God Reveals My "Husbae" In A Dream 50

Ch. 6 | Discovering My Parents...................58
            Planning The 2nd Annual "Walk By Faith" Conference (2017) 63

Ch. 7 | 365 Days Of Loving Me.....................65
            All Nations Worship Assembly - Chicago Campus 68

Ch. 8 | Family Ties...73

Ch. 9 | Supernatural Publishing..................82

Ch. 10 | Hearing God During Transitions 88

Ch. 11 | The Benefits of Corporate Prayer & Fasting 95

Ch. 12 | I Got SHOT AT! Real Bullets! 97

Ch. 13 | Another FREE Venue 105

Ch. 14 | The 2nd Annual "Walk By Faith" Conference 107

Ch. 15 | God Called Me To Entrepreneurship ... 110

Ch. 16 | A Starbucks Barista. Oh, Lord! 115

Ch. 17 | I'm Going Going, Back Back To Cali, Cali 124

THE
DEEPER THINGS

BLIND FAITH Vol. 2

JOURNAL ENTRY

Wed. June 29th 2016
"Worst Cooks in America
Semi-Finalist"

So, I'm laying down reading in Lancaster, CA. I get a call from "Worst Cooks in America" casting. It was a women by the name of _____. She said that I was selected as a semi-finalist and that she will be my point of contact from now on. She asked if I would be available. I said yes. She said she would send me an email and to follow all directions in the email. In this moment I'm super excited and ready. God if this is a door you opening for me I'll take it! Just go before me and protect me where ever my feet tread. I love you God!!

> *He fills my life with good things, so that I stay young and strong like an eagle.*
>
> PSALM 103:5

July 17th DAY 1 WCA
Flight → NYC!

Lord, I don't know what to think! All I can do is trust you. You are definitely putting my "FAITH" to work. I'm not scared though, just wondering "what the heck" La are you up there doing!? BUT I trust you. And I'm excited about WCA! Let's go win God and impact like never before! Make me alert! Allow my eyes to be open. Don't make me defensive, sarcastic, angry or impatient! God work through me in the mighty name of Jesus"! Let your light shine! I love you God! Thank you for loving me! So, I

Chapter 1
Flewed (Flown) Out to NYC

i made it to New York City, baby! Who would have thought that this girl from Dolton, Illinois would be "flewed" (flown) out for free and starring on a national television show: "Worst Cooks in America." Not me. A side note: Honestly, I was homeless. Initially, I only took this opportunity because it guaranteed me a place to stay, food and showers. I was looking for some form of stability, and I got just that.

I left my car with a friend in California for the time that I was gone. She was taking the bus every day. So, I thought that leaving my car with her would be a good thing to do since we both needed help for a little while. It's hard taking the bus and train in L.A. The transportation system isn't as efficient as New York City or Chicago, but it will do. I added my friend to my car insurance just in case anything happened while I was away while she had possession of my vehicle. The process was easy. Thank you, Liberty Mutual Insurance. When I had this insurance company, they always helped me and took care of me.

Ah, I landed in New York; and I was picked up in an all-black Suburban truck. Y'all, I was like dang! Okay. They did ya girl right. I have never experienced such service in my life, well, maybe one time when I studied abroad in Rome, Italy; but it wasn't like this. That's an entirely different topic. Anywho, a male driver picked me up. He got out of the car, picked up my bags and opened my door for me. I was in such a beautiful headspace. I felt like a queen. I felt like royalty, similar to the movie *Coming To America*, which is one of my favorite movies, by the way. I was so happy. You guys, I was just in a homeless situation; and God pulled me out and elevated me that quickly. He rescued me from the pits of hell literally.

So, the driver was super nice; and he had hecka snacks in the armrest of the back seat. That was super clutch. We were driving for a while, having a great conversation; and, low-key, I was getting a free tour of the Big Apple.

We arrived in Brooklyn to a location that I still don't know the address to. LOL. As part of my agreed-upon contract, I could not disclose certain information or have my cell phone. Yes. Lawd, they took our phones for the entire summer. Imagine that! You guys in this generation wouldn't know what to do. LOL. Thankfully, God blessed me with the beautiful gift that I use quite often. I'm a social butterfly. I can talk to anybody.

Okay. So, I walked up to the loft apartment; and in I walked into a room full of all kinds of people from different nationalities. They were old, young, male, female and from several different states. It seems like everyone knew who I was, especially the "mom-and-pop" of the house, who were definitely New Yorkers. I mean, man, their accents were so thick. I loved it. I didn't know if I was going to be cool with them or not. They were Black people, but I definitely wasn't feeling how they were talking to me initially. In about a week, we were super cool. I had to learn the way they interacted with one another and with others. I went into straight observation mode. That was just how they were.

We all shared some cultural differences to begin with. Everybody was trying to feel each other out. However, over time, we were like a family, like on the rooftop chilling almost every night, laughing and getting to know each other like back in the olden days. There was a time in history where people actually sat down and paid attention to each other. We were so concerned about each other's well-being, how we were raised and shared common childhood stories with each other to reassure each other that we were not in this thing we called life alone. It was everything for me not to have a phone. You can take me just about anywhere for a week or two and tell me I can't use my phone and I would be so happy, LOL, for real. Yeah. So, those late nights on the roof were so fun.

But granny over here, yes, I'm referring to myself, would dip on them too quickly. We had to be up hecka early to get to set. We had long 12-hour days of filming, interviewing and learning how to cook. Yo, that can get exhausting and tiresome on the body real quick. As soon as we would cut to go home, I used to be super thirsty. I was one of the first ones on the van to head back, but not in the AM. That scenario would be reversed. LOL.

What I will say is that production made sure that we ate, though. And I mean we ate good. I think this is the only time in my adult life that I legitimately ate three meals a day, except when I was a child. We ordered whatever we wanted every day. Like, *"How Sway?"* I can order whatever I want? Let me tell y'all, this baby girl right here gained well over 20 pounds. I didn't realize how big I was until I saw the pictures we took at the end of the summer.

I digress. So, it's time to shoot the commercial for our season, Season 10 of "Worst Cooks in America." Initially when shooting the commercial, I did not have a speaking role. However, somebody wasn't ready. You know that saying "Stay ready so you don't have to get ready?" Oh, yeah, that was me. I was ready, ready in my Tiffany Haddish voice. One of the directors came from the other room and asked me to say, "You can't make a smoothie with that." So, I did just that; and he loved it. He gave me the line one more time and instructed me to add a little more facial expression to it and told me to say it again. So, I said the line again the exact same way he did; and I killed, killed, murdered, murdered and destroyed it. LOL. He then gave me another line to say but with a very dramatic look on my face and a suggestive tone: "It does?"

Let's just say when the commercial finally aired, that part of the commercial was highlighted. It felt so good to get all the text messages, DMs on social media and phone calls about seeing me on TV. I told nobody that I would be on TV. I had so many people weak (laughing hard) at me just playing the role of myself. I tend to believe that I am a naturally funny/goofy person. Now the whole world knows it.

You know what, though? I did a lot of self-reflecting while I was in NYC. It was good for me, and I needed that. I also knew that I was there on an assignment from God and to get peace of mind for myself. Mainly the entire time I was there, I spent my time ministering the Gospel, prophesying and being a beacon of light. I developed some very unique relationships while I was there and experienced some things that you just can't unsee or unhear. It's called life.

Whenever I would get frustrated during my interviews because of the long hours, I would ask my producer for a three-minute break. I would put on my worship music and take that time to be filled up by God. In that, most of the time, the camera guys would still be recording me. I legit would have to get my God time in wherever I was. I spent so much time in the presence of the Holy Spirit that when I don't get my QT (quality time is my love language with

God), I am super annoyed and moody. The entire taping experience was pretty epic, though. I will get into this a little later on in the book.

> 2016 "elimination"
>
> So today, I cooked my last WCA meal. I had no idea I was going home. I'm the best cook there. Like, Idk what Cheft was thinking. She gave me all good feedback then told me to go home. I didn't cry doe! La Imma g! I just smiled and said thank you and gave hugs and dabbed Ann. She my ___ She has to win! So, I had to do on interview. Then finish my previous interviews. I was trying but then I got tired and semi-annoyed. I'm like what the heck Rach. So, Rach tells me knock out 30 more minutes cuz she has a surprise for me. So I zoom thraught it and she tells me "Yo mom is waiting for you at the hotel"! I knew she was there. God told me but I acted surprise but I was really happy.

8 | Flewed (Flown) Out to NYC

Guess what, y'all? They flew my momma out to NYC. The crazy thing is I got eliminated that same day. LOL. I am so glad that my mom was there during a time like that. To think about it, my mom has never missed a moment of comfort when I needed it the most. God always made sure she was there and continues to be there. We lived our best life while in NYC before we headed back to Chicago.

Okay. Real quick, a funny story: So, my mom and I were walking in NYC's Time Square; and she was a bit farther up than I was, trying to buy peanuts. I lagged behind, searching for souvenirs. So, when I walked up, my mom was angry because the man was giving her a hard time about the price of the peanuts. The guy was a middle-aged, Middle Eastern man whose back was towards me this entire time.

You guys, this man turns around; and he looks at me as if he's seeing his childhood idol. I mean his mouth was wide open, eyes big as day and screaming in a high-pitched voice, "Just take the peanuts, take them." He then says, "Oh, my God. You are so gorgeous." I didn't know what to do. I was just in shock myself. My mom was looking at me in awe with her mouth open as well while taking the peanuts out of the man's hands. LOL. I was blushing so hard. I told the man "Thank you," and I walked away.

I was blown away. And then I heard a small voice say, "You are beautiful." God has a funny way of bringing you out of agreement with negative thoughts about yourself. It's not that I don't think I am beautiful, but sometimes you just don't feel your best all the time. But as I have traveled outside of my own city, state and country, I constantly get approached and stopped by men and women who think that I am so gorgeous. I'll take that.

Okay. One more small story that I want to tell only because I like to gas (boast, pump, brag) on myself sometimes. LOL. There was this other time while in NYC on a rest break from shooting a commercial where we were walking across a major intersection with a stoplight. There was this tall, 6'4", light-skinned, sexy man walking towards me. He was fine, fine and just the way I liked them. Well, on the exterior anyway. He was walking with a young lady by his side. So, I didn't think twice after that because I assumed that was his lady.

But, when he got closer to me, in the middle of the intersection, he grabs my hand, looks me in the eyes, smiles at me and says, "You are so gorgeous." Y'all, I could not breathe. It felt like something from a movie. I smiled and said, "Thank you." And we parted ways. Instantly, of course all the girls with me were yelling at me, saying "Why didn't you get his number? He was so attractive." I'm like, chill. LOL. If he wanted my number, he would have asked for it. Plus, it's not like I would ever see him again because we were filming and on a tight schedule.

In other news, God whispered to me again: "I am going to keep reminding you of what I think about you until you get it." That was the point of the interaction; nothing else.

Oh, you guys, remember my roommate no. 2 in my previous book, *Blind Faith*, where I told the story of how my roommate wanted to pay my portion of the rent because she said that she felt like God was telling her to? So, while I was in New York, I received a deposit to my account for $948.00. The money came from my insurance company. On the 4th of July, 2016, someone broke into my car and stole all of my things. When I was homeless, I stayed at my neighbor's house for the night. And the next day, I had to go audition for an AT&T commercial. Well, this was the refund check for the property that was taken from me.

It's so important to have a car and renters' insurance for this very reason. It's very inexpensive. Look into insurance companies and make sure you cover yourself for unforeseen circumstances that may come about. The insurance company that I had at the time was Liberty Mutual. They were really good.

Now, back to what I was saying. All of my bills were paid, and I didn't know what to do with the money. So, I asked God what He wanted me to do; and He whispered my roommate's name in my ear. His voice was so clear. I had almost forgotten that I owed that girl money. It legit slipped my mind because of all that was going on. See, God will bring things back to your memory. That's what I love about God. He's got your back fo' sho', fo' sho'. So, I reached out to my roommate no. 2 and paid her my portion of the rent that she covered for me earlier than she expected to be paid, literally a whole month earlier. Look at God!

The Deeper Things | 13

TUE 8/23/16

"Rapid Rewards points"

So I woke up expecting God for some direction. So I asked him "Lord tell me what to do". He said go back to where you came from. I'm like Lord but I have no place to go or a job. He said, Do you trust me. I said yea. He said I have already provided for you Brittany. Just know I felt nervousness and fear all over again just like when I first left to go to L.A. I had nothing but I booked my flight on faith. So now I remembered and said ok. I know I have bills to pay and didn't think I would have enough to pay for it all. So I tried to access my Southwest rewards info but it said it was wrong. So I called the lady and she explained how to use my points. So I asked God what day he said, Aug 30 and book the 3 o'clock flight so I did. I saw that I had 7,200 points. So I booked that flight for 6,500 points and look at God! I only had to pay $5.10 for my flight! I'm like okay God on purpose. I see you. So I'm

Chapter 2
Misshapes & Miracles

i returned back to Los Angeles to find that my car was in major disrepair. I thought that my car just needed some minor work done on it. No! Y'all, my car was riding like it had been in an accident. There was no way that my car should have sounded the way it did, nor should it have been driving the way it was. I had no money to pay for my car to be fixed, and that was my only possession. It was technically my house. I was still homeless in L.A., couch-hopping and sleeping in my car. I could not believe that my car was broken.

The friend whom I let borrow my car initially was not going to even offer to help me. While away, I even told her to connect with one of my brothers in Christ so that he could fix it. That never happened. My car wasn't even drivable. Yo, it was ridiculous. We talked about it, and I just gave her the benefit of the doubt. She wasn't in a position to offer anything financially. However, I did express to her how insensitive her initial reaction was.

She explained to me what her thought process was regarding that matter as well. It was all good.

So, here I am praying that God will help me. So, the next day, I heard the Lord say the name of a tire place that I once went to before to get my tires done. I want you to keep in mind that I had no money, and I was moving in faith according to what I heard the Lord say to me. So, I go to the tire place. There was a Black woman working there. I was shocked to see her because mainly Hispanics worked there. I explained to the lady that my car was messed up and that I wanted to see if they could do a diagnostic test on my car. So, she took the chart to the back and told me to have a seat.

While waiting for two hours and not even realizing it, I ministered to a couple of people in the lobby. First, it was a woman who was feeling discouraged about a few things in her life. I simply shared a few stories of my own where I too was feeling discouraged. And somehow, the stories that I shared with her turned out to be her exact situation too. Hmm. I wonder what the odds of that was. God is so funny and timely; it makes no sense. Some people would call it odd or a coincidence. I call it a dope prophetic gift. The woman was so happy and encouraged and excited to share this news with her husband. I absolutely love talking about God.

After my conversation with the woman in the waiting room, the Black lady at the desk returned and told me that hecka (a lot) stuff was wrong with my car. I needed a wheel alignment, rotors, brakes and three new tires. I was overwhelmed. I expressed to the lady that I could not afford that. She told me to have a seat and to wait a minute. So, I did.

Next, I began to talk to an older White male in the waiting room. He started talking to me about Jesus. In the midst of our conversation, he says, "Can you slow down talking. I'm reading your lips." His request caught me off guard. The entire time, he could not really hear what I was saying. He said that he was waiting on his hearing aids to come in the mail. I was moved with compassion for him, just like Jesus was for the multitude.

> *The Bible says, "When Jesus landed and saw a large crowd, He had compassion on them and healed their sick." Matthew 14:14 (NIV).*

I asked him, "Would you like for me to pray for you?" He said, "Sure." He got out of his seat quickly and came and sat down in the seat beside me. There were many people in the lobby, including the Black lady who worked there. Unashamed in faith, I stood behind him and placed a hand on each one of his ears. I closed my eyes and began to pray what I heard in the spirit. When I was done praying, I asked him how he felt. I noticed that his face was really red. I asked him, "Is everything all right?" He said, "I could hear the moment you started praying for me." He said it with such excitement and shock. I was so happy because I didn't know what he was going to say. God worked a miracle on that day, and not just one but two.

A few minutes later, the gentleman left; and the Black lady came from the back. She said, "Okay, sign here and here." I was hesitant, and I began to notice that I was signing documents that had huge prices on them. I said, "Ma'am." And she interrupted me and said, "You were a blessing. Now receive your blessing. It's on me." Y'all, I instantly began to cry and hugged her so tight and said thank you like a hundred times. She handed me my keys and said, "Keep on being a blessing." I walked outside.

And as they pulled my car out, I just started screaming "THANK YOU, JESUS" over and over again. God never fails me. He always shows up on time.

> *1 Thessalonians 5:24 says, "He who calls you is faithful; He will surely do it" (ESV).*

Chapter 3
Location, Location, Location

By this time, I am still in a homeless situation; but I'm not really complaining. I am just adjusting to my circumstance so I won't be so irritated. However, I just found out that my mom is coming to Cali for the first time to visit my auntie for her birthday. I guess that means I am taking a trip to Northern California. So, a few weeks later, I met my mother in California. I mean the whole family was there. The whole family flew out from Chicago. It had to be like 30 of us. We were deep (meaning a large group of people). My auntie is a constant reminder that God is a miracle worker. She wasn't even supposed to live to see 60. She has lived with a pacemaker in her heart for over half of her life. She now has had many heart surgeries and is living with the use of a defibrillator and has a stronger heart. You go, auntie! She is a fighter, y'all.

When I tell you that my uncle, her husband, is the real MVP to this marriage thing, he is. Her children love her to death, and she is spoiled and I mean spoiled. LOL. My future husband better spoil me like my uncle spoils my auntie. She had an entire Italian ice truck for her birthday. She went all out. Y'all can't tell me we don't serve a good God.

> *James 1:17 says, "Every good and perfect gift is from above, coming down from the Father of heavenly lights, who does not change like shifting shadows" (NIV).*

We had a Onesie-themed pajama sleepover. Everyone looked so cute in their sleepwear. My auntie teamed up with my Mommie, and they sprayed everybody with Silly String. My cousins were running up and down the stairs, in the kitchen and in the living room. It was just a good time. We are a family of Christians. So, of course, my aunt wanted all of us to participate in a family talent show. Of course, she asked me to praise dance. I didn't want to because I hadn't danced in years. I did it anyway because, like I said before, my auntie is spoiled. Let's just say the Holy Spirit took over my body. It was beautiful.

Another one of my aunts and some cousins shared with me that at the end of my dance, they saw an angel open his wings over me. My aunt said, "God is with you, Brittany." I couldn't believe what I was hearing. I was looking for the angel, and I couldn't see him. Some people are born with the ability to see evil spirits or angels from birth. Other people can develop the gift upon intimacy with the Holy Spirit or if God feels like allowing your eyes to see them. Y'all, I really want to see angels. I'm quite fascinated with the idea of it. However, I know that if God gives me the ability to see angels, then I will see demons. I ain't on that. Yo' girl doesn't even like scary movies. LOL. However, when the time comes, I will be more than ready.

> *In 2 Kings 6:16-17, the Bible says, "Don't be afraid," the prophet answered. "Those who are with us are more than those who are with them." And Elisha prayed, "Open his eyes, Lord, so that he may see." The Lord opened the servant's eyes, and he looked and saw the hills full of horses and chariots of fire all around Elisha (NIV).*

You guys have to go and read this story in the Bible on your own. Elisha was a dope prophet and operated in such a unique anointing. He is by far one of my favorite prophets in the Bible.

Later on in the evening, a woman comes in with her sister. These women looked like average women attending the birthday party like everyone else. I remember I was praying for the family as a whole. After I got done praying, one of the women started prophesying to me and going in (continuous decrees over my life). I never had anyone be that specific with me in a prophecy. I remember thinking who is this lady? Oh, she is definitely a prophet. I don't toss titles around just because you gave me an accurate Word. I felt it in my Spirit Man. I mean the Word was powerful. Her boldness to release the Word of God allowed our gifts to be activated. It became like a tag team in the Spirit. Everybody was prophesying.

I watched as my mom received her prophecy, and I wasn't too sure that my mom had experienced anything like that before. The most significant thing in my mother's prophecy was the way God feels about her. My personal observation of my mom's prophecy was that my Mommie is our Heavenly Father's daughter first, and then she's my mother secondly. Her prophecy almost took me out. I was so grateful that God didn't allow my mom to come all the way to California and not allow her to have an encounter with Him. I said, "God, if you have done all these great things for me here in Cali, do it for her." That was my prayer on my four-hour drive up to Northern California from Southern California. And He answered my prayer.

Thankfully, the party was everything my aunt wanted and more. I am so happy that she and the family had an amazing time. The night before I left, one of my little cousins was talking to me about the prophecy I received about being married soon from the prophet. Let's say we are going to talk about the timing of God and the consequences of my disobedience a little later, okay? I just have to be honest with myself and you all. Yes, little ol' me was disobedient. It's not often that I am, but I wanted to be petty and hasty. So, after some dialogue, my cousin said, "you said something along the lines of light-skinned? I saw you with a dark-skinned man as your husband."

Y'all remember "The Boo" from the first book? Well,

we were still dating off and on. I know, I know, guys. Why am I still dealing with him and I'm all the way in Cali? I loved him, y'all. Dang. LOL. That's why. He was my comfort, and I'd rather take the good times we shared over the bad. I was definitely battling the spirit of loneliness. I knew I should have left him alone.

Anywho, it's the next morning and I am hugging and kissing my Mommie good-bye. Ain't nothing like your mother. You only get one, so cherish her. I don't care what has happened. Honor your parents. They are humans just like us, and they make mistakes. Just think. You will be a parent one day too. Would you want your children to hate you? Who said you are going to get parenting right? See, you don't know the results. You can claim that you will do X-Y and Z; but you don't know fully until you are a parent. So, forgive your parents in your heart and let God do the mending and comforting.

I left my mom knowing that I would be living my life literally day by day.

> *The Bible says, in Matthew 6:34, "Therefore, do not worry about tomorrow, for tomorrow will*

> *worry about itself. Each day has enough trouble of its own" (NIV).*

Thankfully, I had friends at the time who allowed me to stay at their home on certain days. There was this one time during transitioning that a good friend at the time did something so unbelievable and unforgettable. One night, I was going to sleep in Studio City, California, way up in the mountains, where I prayed all the time. I expressed that to her, and she met me at the mountains. She got out of her car and got in my truck and fell asleep with me that night. Man, just her being there with me was so comforting. I had never had anybody throughout my entire homeless experience join me in my journey and walk in my shoes when they didn't have to. It was almost the same experience that Jesus had when Simon from Cyrene beared (carried) the cross with Him on his way to be crucified.

> *In Matthew 27:32, the Bible states that, "Now as they came out, they found a man of Cyrene, Simon by name. Him they compelled to bear His cross" (NKJV).*

I believe that Simon didn't mind carrying Jesus' cross. But being submissive to the soldiers, he had no choice, even if he wanted one. In my situation, she was willing to endure this part of the journey with me. That was an honorable sacrifice, and it proved the position of her heart.

> *The Bible also says in Proverbs 19:17, "Whoever is kind to the poor lends to the LORD, and He will reward them for what they have done" (NIV).*

She made sure I was good all the time; and she even brought me her thick, fancy, clean, white comforter (duvet) that she took off her bed and gave it to me so I wouldn't get too cold in my car. Who does that? The compassion and love that this girl had for people was beyond me. She taught me so much in those moments of need. In that moment, she was my friend, a true definition of friendship. Words cannot express to this day how much her support means to me. THANK YOU again, my friend.

Now, I have stayed from place to place as much as I could. I never wanted to go to a shelter because I didn't think that my situation was that bad. Plus, I had a car. The thought of going to a shelter was gut-wrenching to me. I thought that if I went to a shelter, then that was the bottom, bottom; and I wasn't having it. There is nothing wrong with a shelter because, by all means, if that's what you have to do to stay afloat, then do it.

In my case, I saw too many movies about staying in a shelter and the experiences you go through while you are there. Plus, Will Smith did one hell of a job in that movie *The Pursuit of Happyness* for me to believe every bit of it. He is one of my absolute favorite actors, by the way. I did not have to live out any of those moments, thank God.

However, I did end up staying at a place called The Dream Center in Los Angeles for two weeks. The Dream Center is a faith-based charitable organization. Its mission is to connect broken people to a community of support by offering free resources and services that address immediate and long-term needs in the areas of poverty, addiction and abuse. The Dream Center serves as a resource center focused on finding solutions to homelessness, hunger and the lack of education through residential and community outreach programs (dreamcenter.org).

I stayed in a room with a young lady from the Middle East. She was a Muslim but didn't really know why she believed

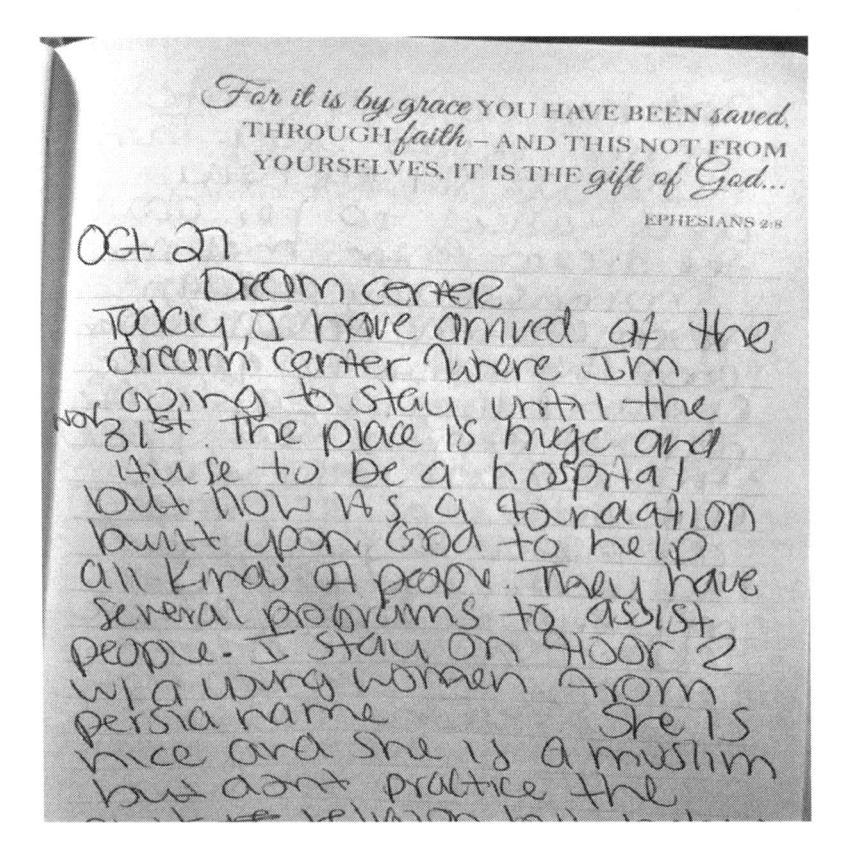

> *For it is by grace* YOU HAVE BEEN *saved*, THROUGH *faith* – AND THIS NOT FROM YOURSELVES, IT IS THE *gift of God*...
> EPHESIANS 2:8
>
> Oct 27
> Dream Center
> Today, I have arrived at the dream center where I'm going to stay until Nov 31st. The place is huge and used to be a hospital but now is a foundation built upon God to help all kinds of people. They have several programs to assist people. I stay on floor 2 w/ a young woman from Persia name ___. She is nice and she is a muslim but don't practice the

the faith that she did. She was super sweet and in America studying to get her bachelor's. Her customs were very interesting to me. I remember when she told me that if a father has a daughter and he passes away and she is unmarried, then the company that he worked for is responsible for taking care of her. I thought that was very interesting and extremely helpful. In other countries, they have systems in place that are beneficial to its citizens. I really enjoy learning about other nationalities and their customs.

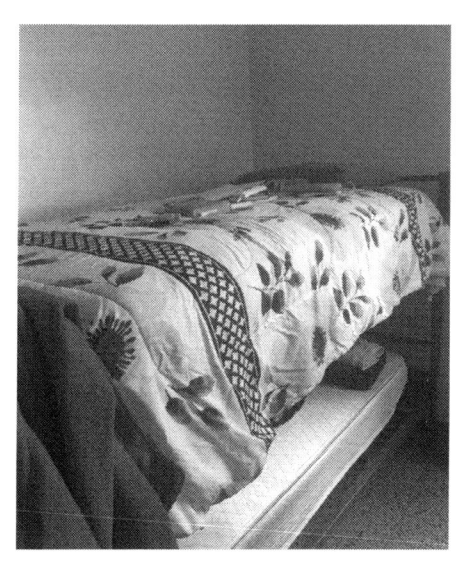

When I was at the Dream Center, I was able to have consistent meals. I didn't have to pay for anything, and the facility reminded me of a university setting. It had communal showers. I was at peace while I was there; and I was able to focus, relax and write my first "*Blind Faith*" book. I was so grateful that the administrative staff had agreed to let me stay there. I met a Ghanaian man while I was there. He worked on computers and had come to the U.S. many years ago. At the time he was planning on traveling back home. And, of course, I encouraged him, especially since he had family there. He was a very nice man. I would speak to him casually as I walked along the facility's walk paths and parking lots.

One evening, I was praying to God about clarity and direction. The Dream Center had a chapel on-site where you could go in and pray. That evening, I was seeking the Lord for direction; and I was just praying and weeping. It feels so good to me to be at the feet of the Lord. His presence is like a comforting blanket to me. It's the safest and most secure place for me in any given situation. When I don't get enough time or when someone is interrupting my time with God, I get so angry and annoyed. You guys, it's not even funny. I love talking to Jesus!

So, the next morning when I woke up, I heard the name of the prophetess that I met at my aunt's birthday party in Northern California. I gave her a call; and she prayed with me and gave me the Word of the Lord, which was to call my aunt and uncle to see if I could come and stay with them. I really didn't want to go stay with my aunt and uncle because I felt as if they had enough people in their home already. They were and have been foster parents for over 20 years now. I just didn't want to be a burden to them. If I could be honest, I felt as if I was grown and shouldn't be in this predicament in the first place.

But I believe everything I was doing, God was ordering my steps and working things out for me. I have so much faith in God. I like to believe that I have radical faith. People probably think I'm crazy, but I cannot unsee what I have seen the Lord do in my life. Does that make sense? Let me explain. I have developed such a deep relationship with God that nobody can tell me that He isn't real. It's just like working out.

Okay. So, for those of you who go to the gym and work out and follow a diet plan, if you stick to the plan for a few months and start to see results, nine times out of ten, you are going to continue with that workout method and diet plan; right? Right. That's how I would explain my relationship with Christ. My faith in Him just works even though I may experience pain, tiredness, doubt, insecurity and even the feeling of giving up, just like all the emotions that come from working out for most people. I choose to keep pushing and cultivating the relationship because I want to continue to see the results that come from being consistent and disciplined.

> *Therefore, if anyone is in Christ, HE IS a new creation; THE OLD HAS GONE, THE NEW has come!*
> — 2 CORINTHIANS 5:17

NOV 15 2016

Today I took a trust leap. I moved to ↓ I don't know what God is up too. He told me to go so I did. I got instruction to move before I actually paid attention. I had to get out of my own way, to do it God's way. Even until this point I still found myself placing limits on God. In this more I can truly say that I am submitted to his will. I asked God to move me into a big house w/ my own room and pay no rent. He did just that. He moved me to my aunti big house. LOL! God is funny

After some time with battling the spirit of pride, I called my auntie and asked her if I could come and live with her. My auntie loves her some Britt Britt. So, of course she said yes. It was my plan to head there just in time for Thanksgiving. I stayed with my aunt and uncle for a little over a month just before going home for Christmas. A funny thing happened while I was there. My uncle couldn't find his wallet. So, he asked me to help him look for it. The house was so big, the wallet could have been anywhere. Y'all know the first thing I did was call on the Holy Spirit to help me. Why would I make my job harder if God said He is a present help?

> *According to John 14:26, the Bible says, "But the Helper, the Holy Spirit, whom the Father will send in My name, He will teach you all things,*

> *and bring to your remembrance all that I said to you" (NASB).*

Well, help me then, Lord. LOL. I heard the Lord say, "The bedroom." I told my uncle it's in your room. He said that he looked there. So, I went up to his and my aunt's room and began to look for it. Then I heard the Lord say "Closet." So, I looked there. At first, I didn't see anything. I asked my uncle did he change pants, and he said yeah. So, we looked for the pants; and nothing was in them. However, I kept hearing the Lord say "Closet." I began to look again. My mom used to always say, "bend your back" whenever she asked us to look for anything, LOL, as if we weren't looking hard enough. And I did just that.

I got on my hands and knees and began moving stuff around where my uncle's pants were on the floor. Would y'all imagine that? I found the wallet. I was so proud. My chest was all poked out like a superhero. LOL. I was happy that I used my ability to hear from the Lord to find my uncle's wallet. With the biggest grin on my face, I told my uncle I found it. He said, "Where was it?" I said, "In the closet, just where God told me it was." He smiled and said, "Thank you." My uncle has a very flint face all the time, and he hardly smiles. But he is the sweetest guy you will ever meet. I love you, unc.

Let's look at this analogy, though. God places me in places for many reasons. It can be for something big or small. In this case, God used me to solve a problem. One of my professional strengths is problem solving. God will use what's naturally down on the inside of you to help solve a problem. Ask God to place you where you can meet the needs of others by solving problems that requires one of your natural abilities. This will help you feel more purposeful, whether that is at work, church, school, volunteering, helping your family or community. I know you may be thinking that was a big analogy from that small situation, but that is how I think. Welcome to my world. I challenge you to come up higher and think as the Lord does. He is always showing us something and putting us in various predicaments to grow in our faith and relationship with Him.

Now it's time to head home to Chicago. It's lit! I miss my Mommie. Meanwhile, I left my little red 1997 Honda CR-V truck in front of my aunt and uncle's house while I was away. I knew it would be safe there.

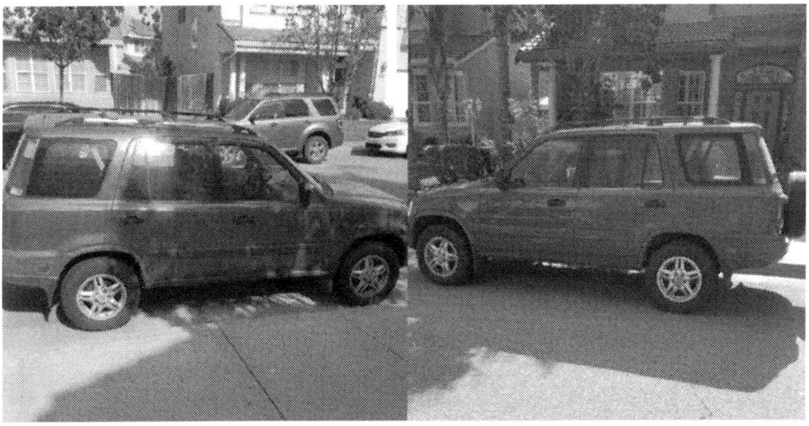

Chapter 4
Home For The Holidays

*b*ack in the Chi. And guess who is here? Bran Bran. He is now in Downtown Chicago until he is moved to Minnesota to do the remainder of his time. For those of you who don't know and have not read *Blind Faith*, my first book, you are in violation. Stop reading now and go read my first book. LOL. My brother has been in federal custody for some time now. I have not seen my twin in so long, I'm too thirsty (really excited).

One weekend, I took my twin's goddaughter to see him. She hadn't seen him in a long time, and her Bran is her favorite. It's super cold, mind you. And we are catching the Metra train all the way Downtown from the South Suburbs of Chicago. They don't call it the Windy City for no reason. We were getting smacked by those cold winds. So, we finally made it to the facility. We get to the federal jail, and they had a list of what we couldn't wear or bring inside. However, I would say that the federal facility is much more inviting than the county facility. The County Jail treats visitors like inmates. They make it hard for us so that we refuse to come back and visit our loved ones. NOT GONNA HAPPEN, CAPTAIN! Nothing in this world is going to stop me from seeing my twin period!

I encourage anyone that has a loved one that is incarcerated to go see them, write them letters, send them books and magazines and put money on their books, etc. It's hard enough behind those walls and even harder when you don't have anyone to "do the time with you," as my twin would say. I know that this is a topic that could be controversial. With that being said, forgive and let go. Being isolated and going through trials, God knows that what's behind those walls are punishment enough. Allow God to heal you from past pain and hurt from your loved one who is behind bars. God is taking care of them, and He knows where it will hurt them the most. Don't you go playing God.

> *Proverbs 3:11 says, "My child, don't reject the Lord's discipline, and don't be upset when He corrects you" (NLT).*

So anyway, we go through the whole security process

and are finally on the elevator going up to see Bran. We finally make it up, and we are escorted to the waiting room. There are plenty of tables and seats, a few vending machines and a children's area. Oh. If you ever want to go visit your family member, bring at least $10 in singles so that you can get everybody something to eat. Keep in mind that when you visit them, a vending machine meal is probably the best meal they will get for a while.

    Next, we hear the alarm. That lets us and the officers know that the inmates are behind the doors. The doors open, and everyone is hastily looking for their loved one. Y'all know my twin walks out with the biggest grin, wearing a crispy clean two-piece green jail outfit and his Ray-Ban glasses. I let his goddaughter give him a hug first. She couldn't stop smiling and staring at him. Y'all know me. I gave this man the tightest hug and instantly started cracking jokes about how clean he was, his name brand glasses, crisp haircut and his chunkiness. LOL. We laughed so hard during our visit, and it was just a great time. We stayed maybe two hours, I think, and then headed back home. It's always hard leaving my twin. That's my boy. Y'all don't understand. That's my son. Ha-ha. He's going to kill me for this because he always says he's my daddy. Ahh, the things we say to each other.

But nawh, for real, for many years, my twin has been my priority, my headache, my friend, my supporter and my heartbreak. He is everything to me. I watched this man go through so much. His strength is beyond me, and I'm a pretty strong person. I just love him. Furthermore, "Worst Cooks in America" is about to air. And guess who gets to watch it? Bran. He said he was going to make them turn to the show so that everybody could watch it.

WATCH PARTY NIGHT

So many people have been tagging me on social media and re-posting the commercials on their pages. I received so many random DMs expressing how proud they were of me; and, of course, flattering DM's stating how fine I looked on TV. That's what the males were saying. That's why they were going to watch the show. I was so weak, LOL. It's all love, and I'm here for it.

It's January 1, 2017; and my homeboy from college, who is a distinguished gentleman of Alpha Phi Alpha Fraternity, Inc., threw me a watch party at his house. It was a small gathering; but yet, it was so much fun. We had lots of food and refreshments. And my momma was there. It was so weird seeing myself on TV. Like, I'm always re-watching my videos that I record on social media for my tribe. But this was different, and I think it was because I didn't know how they would edit the show or what type of person or character they would portray me as. I was nervous and excited all at the same time.

I know they wouldn't play me, though, because I wasn't going. I remember my producer wanted me to say a few corny lines, and I wouldn't say them. I told her that back home, I'm not a cornball or a lame; I'm popular, and people will know you made me say these corny lines.

LOL. I'm telling y'all I was not playing with her. She would always laugh at me, but I was dead serious. So, it's funny now, thinking back on it. She was super cool.

I even remember having a cocky moment, if I can be honest. I am going to keep it as 100 as I possibly can with y'all, okay? I am not perfect, and I have grown so much over the past several years. I had been praying to God to take my pettiness away, LOL; but there's still some inside of me. Most importantly, I think that's why I still have some friends and family who claim "not to be all the way saved" for this reason. I think this is the funniest crap ever.

Back to my cocky moment that stemmed from a little pain and unforgiveness that I was dealing with, I had an internal moment that went something like this: Yeah. For every dude that has ever done me bogus is gonna be salty that I'm on TV. And this ain't gonna be the end of it. They're gonna have to watch me on the screen for the rest of their lives. Why was this even a thought? Because some part of me wanted revenge for how they treated me. But, in my way, this would be how it would manifest. At the time, I had never taken personal revenge on someone. I always let God do it because that's what His

Word says.

The desire to even want them to remember what they did to me revealed so much more healing and forgiveness that I had to go through. The process isn't easy, and that is why most of us don't go through it. We either take matters into our own hands, or we carry bitterness and hate in our hearts. That's honestly what makes us sick and causes us to rely on other things to help with the pain. We self-medicate the pain with sex, drugs, alcohol, shutting people out, isolating ourselves, depression, etc. We've got to let it go. For me, the way I felt was real because they will not see the end of me on TV. But my intentions on why I wanted them to see me was wrong, so I allowed myself to officially start my healing process.

Chapter 5
Switching Lanes

"Worst Cooks in America" is still airing, and I am still getting so much clout. I interviewed on so many news stations in Chicago, and I'm loving the space that I'm in and still living my regular old life. I went to see my twin brother again, and he told me that he watched the show and that he liked it. It's always good to get his feedback because he will never sugarcoat anything for me.

By this time, I am subbing (substitute teaching) in my hometown at the schools I attended growing up in and even teaching in my rivalry schools.

I was a very athletic person growing up. It was healthy and fun rivalry, though not what these kids are doing nowadays, which is out of control. I digress. I will address that another time or later on in this book if I feel like it. I found myself becoming a regular sub during this time because the kids loved me. I mean who wouldn't love Ms. Moore? I engaged the children and youth and talked about real-life situations. I was able to see what their barriers were in school and what social and emotional challenges they were facing inside and outside of school. I also was able to see how dope, brilliant, talented, creative and smart they all were.

I was one of those subs that managed to get even the most troubled students to do their homework and turn in their assignments. Most of the problem or so-called bad kids are more likely than not the smartest ones. I learned that early on by watching how my twin was in school. The kids aren't bad. They are active, creative and energetic and trying to figure out how to place these emotions or how to articulate them. Nine times out of ten, they are misunderstood; and opportunities are stripped from them instantly. And then they rebel against authority.

I remember when I was subbing in the elementary schools and at the junior high schools, it felt so good to talk to the kids and let them know that I sat in those same seats and that I came from the same community as they did. That made me that much more relatable. It made me even more grateful for my upbringing, my mom, teachers, counselors, deans, play parents, etc. It really does take a village to raise a child. I remember myself as a young girl and all the freedom I had as a kid. I would encourage anybody to go to your old stomping grounds, if the schools are still there, and talk to the kids. They need your insight, care, love, support and, most of all, your story.

The age group that I connected with the most were the 7th-12th graders. They are my babies. I had the pleasure of watching most of them grow from an immature little kid to a maturing young teen. My kids used to bring me candy, buy me lunch and crack jokes on me; and I used to heat (crack jokes back) them too. It was all love, but they knew not to play with me. I always told them I am not a child. I was hard on them because I wanted them to do well, and I know that most of them lacked that support at home for so many reasons.

My God. These kids are going through so much more than I did when I was growing up. So, patience and structure are needed for them to be successful. When I would sub, most teachers would ask me how did you get (no-name) kids to do their work? I simply told them I get on their level, understand them and tell them what I expect of them moving forward. Sometimes it's just in the approach, the tone and the delivery to get them to see your perspective.

    I remember when I subbed at the high school for the first time. Y'all know I still got a baby face, right? LOL. Some of those kids looked older than me. I walked into the classroom and sat down at one of the tables as if I was a student. So, this young man walks in like, "Um, is you new?" I said, "Yeah." He said, "Ahh, I was about to say 'cause you in my seat. But since you new, you can stay." Then he goes on to ask me, "What school you transferred from?" So, I played along. I said, "Thornridge." He said, "Oh? My cousins go to The Ridge." LOL.

    So, this White lady walked in and said, "Where's your sub?" They said, "We don't know." She said, "Well, I'm about to call the office and let them know she or he is not here." I had to raise my voice and say, "You don't have to do that. I'm their sub." By this time, I had talked to almost everybody in the class and got them thinking I was the new girl. Ha-ha! Y'all, they were like "What? You're the sub? You look so young." One of the students replied, "I can tell this class is about to be fun." By the end of the day, I had all kinds of kids coming to my classroom who weren't supposed to be in there; but I let them stay. I'd rather them be in my class doing work than running the hallways and getting into trouble.

It was such an opportune time for me to be back at home and subbing. My students had the opportunity to get to know me and watch me on TV. That was the highlight of their week. They would see me in the halls and blurt out something I said on TV, and all the students would laugh.

Another cool moment was when I was in the cafeteria. I was talking to a young Caucasian female, a Spanish teacher, who was a huge fan of mine from "Worst Cooks in America." I was talking to her. And then, all of a sudden, she turned red. I'm like, "What's wrong? Are you okay?" I'll paraphrase this; but she said something like, Your voice, I knew it sounded familiar. You look different. But now that I'm looking at you, you look the same. You're Brittany Bring-It. My mom and I watch you all the time. You are our favorite on the show. Can you take a selfie with me so I can send it to my mom? My insides were so full. LOL. I was elated to take a photo with her. I legit felt like a celebrity, but not in an idolizing way. These are moments in my life I will simply never forget.

God has used people before to speak into my life way before this experience. They would say things like, "You're going to be famous, you're going to make it big, you're going to be a celebrity, I can see you going far, you have a face for TV," etc. All this simply gave me a peek into my future, and I continue to hold onto the words of the Lord. I actually just read a book called *Marked* by Dr. Faith Wokoma (askdrfaith.com) where she speaks more in-depth about how to identify your purpose through what others have always spoken over you. It is a great book to get if you want to know more about why you were created and why you have experienced certain things in your life.

He Is Still In The Picture: God Reveals My "Husbae" In A Dream

I got home in December of 2016, a few days before Christmas. Of course I stayed in contact with "The Boo." I was back home where things felt normal and things seemed to fall naturally back into place for us. We began to go on dates again, spending a lot of time together and all that. It got to the point of deciding that we wanted to make our relationship official, but something didn't feel right. There were things happening in the natural that looked great. It seemed as if we were moving forward, but my Spirit Man was vexed. It was like a huge warning buzzer flashing on the inside of my body. It's like I felt it and saw it. As the days went by, things still seemed to be going great.

One day, he brought his daughter over to meet me. Well, I met her once before; but this time we actually spent time with one another. This was one of my requirements if we were going to be together. I wasn't going to allow us to have a relationship and I didn't have a relationship with his child nor the mother of his child. I was raised better than that; and, plus, if the tables were turned, I would want that same respect in return. His daughter was so smart; and we got along very well, which I knew that we would.

Remember guys, I had spent a year in Cali developing my relationship with God and developing my spiritual gifts. So, it is extremely difficult to ignore God talking to me. I was sitting on the floor playing with his daughter, and he was sitting on the couch. I looked at him and I heard the word "sneaky." He even physically looked different even though he was smiling at me in the natural. In the spirit, I saw him smirking at me, not smiling. Shortly after that, he left and the baby left. He did not tell me that he would have his daughter. Seeing her let me know his BM (baby's momma) wasn't too far away because he didn't drive to go get his daughter because he was with me the night before. His daughter lived in a nearby state that was some distance away.

Anyway, a week prior to meeting his daughter, I found out he was going to Las Vegas. I asked him who he was going with. He said his cousin and some chicks. Mind you, I have been in L.A.; but I've been home several times during the time I lived in L.A. If anybody is from my neck of the woods, it doesn't matter what was going on when we were apart; we would always pick up right where we left off. This is very toxic behavior, by the way; but I was having a very human moment at this time in my life. We had a conversation about starting fresh and moving forward. So, at this point, I had a right to feel the way I felt.

Okay. So, we were at my friend's house listening to music and socializing. I asked was he still going on the trip. He says no, that he wants me, all of me, so he isn't going. He said he would tell the girl and his cousin he wasn't going anymore. I believed him. What female wouldn't believe her dude? Shorty deserved an Oscar for that act that he put up, man!

So, it's the morning that he supposedly is not going out of town. I am sitting on my momma's couch, and I get an open vision of him at the doggone airport. Y'all, the vision was as clear as day. So, I called this man; and he didn't answer. So, I called him again. No answer. He finally calls me back, and I play it off real cool. I'm like, "Hey, babe, what you doing?" He's like, "Nothing." I'm like, "Well, come get me so we can go eat." He's like, "Um. Um. Um." He's mute. Homeboy is not saying a word. So, I'm like, "Hello?" He's like, "Yeah, I'm here." I'm like, "Why did you get quiet?" He's' like, "'Cause, um. Um." I said, "Because you're about to go to Vegas; and you lied to me." I said, "I don't know why you play with me. I can see in the spirit. God showed me a vision of you at the airport." He said, "I couldn't back out at the last minute."

I was so pissed! I cannot stand a liar. So, I'm like, "So, why do you feel obligated to go all the way to Vegas with some random female and you ain't never flown with me anywhere?" This ninja gets quiet again. Instantly, I heard "baby momma." Then I said, "Unless you lied about the female you're taking, it's your baby's momma that you claim you ain't been messing with." This mug gonna tell me that he started back talking to her while I was away and that they planned the trip a few months ago. But I'm like, "You hate her, though. She makes your life a living hell; but you want to play boyfriend and girlfriend, huh?" Okay. I told that clown to have fun and don't call my phone number anymore. I was heated!

Long story short, because I don't want this book to turn into too much of me talking about him, he comes back to a surprise. LOL. He ended up apologizing to me, and we hung out one last time. In that short time, he tells me he had sex with her, that he did not use a condom and that he just did it just because. He said there were no feelings there. This proves a very valid fact that you shouldn't have sex with a guy to try and make him do anything because sex isn't connected to their emotions. I'm like, "What?" This is too much for me. Then I got a vision of his BM being pregnant, and I heard the word "boy." I told him exactly what I saw and heard and cut him off completely. Even though we never had sex, I was so emotionally caught up in dude that it wasn't even funny. I went into a deep depression for like three weeks.

My momma and a good friend of mine pulled me up out of my depression. Watching a loved one in depression is the most sorrowful thing you can do. I am grateful for them. In this time, I was reminded about what I asked God for before I left Cali. I told God that if "The Boo" was not my husband, then remove him. Let's not forget that this man was prophesied on a few occasions to be my husband. But his fruit just did not add up; and the relationship, the situation, was too hard and painful for God to be in it. The practical way that I came out of depression was going outside and spending more time in social gatherings with my close friends. I began to talk to two other dudes about a month later, just conversation, nothing serious, which turned out not to be the best choice. Oh. And I started hanging out again with one of my good male friends. S/O to OTG! He was fake mad that I didn't put him in my first book. So, here you go, sir. LOL.

A month after the breakup, in January of 2017, I had a very vivid dream about the man I'm supposed to marry. This was the beginning of many regular dreams that I've had and still have over the years concerning him. In the dream, I was with "The Boo." He told me that he wanted to take me to an outing. He told me to go get dressed. All I know is that I was standing in the street in front of some houses and tall three-story brick buildings. The buildings looked very similar to buildings located on the South Side of Chicago. In my dream, I was about to get in my car; and I saw this guy that I had actually encountered from my past. He was a beautiful, Black, dark-skinned man with very distinct features. And I was attracted to him. I never pursued him because I thought that I could never get a guy like him. In my eyes, he was well put together, clean-cut and out of my league. I never viewed a guy in this way before. I always thought that I could get any guy that I wanted, but not him.

This beautiful Black, dark-skinned man walked up to me in this dream and said, "I've been looking for you." All I know is that I was sitting in a hallway, and I was holding a ticket to a masquerade ball. The ticket said that the event was online. And I heard a voice say you are going to have to choose the right one; choose the right way. I was like what? What does this mean?

Then the dude popped up from my past again. So, we were sitting on his couch in the living room. He said, "I've been looking for you." And he had Facebook screenshots of me and my friends on his phone, but I was cut out of the screenshots. They were pictures of what appeared to be half of me, but you could see my friends clearly. Now reflecting, I wasn't a "whole" person with full understanding of my identity, value and self-love.

I had never had a dream like this, nor was I even thinking about the guy from my past that I encountered. I forgot all about him. As months and years have gone by, God continues to give me dreams about him and have even allowed us to come into divine contact periodically. How do I know who my husband is and not be dating him? At first, it was pretty challenging. But right now, it's fairly easy because I have stopped trying to manipulate the situation and let God do his thing. Plus, there is still more work to be done within myself and in him before God brings us together. Until then, I will continue to trust God, pray and decree what He has revealed to me. When this manifests, I'll write an entire book on it. No worries, loves; I got you guys.

Chapter 6
Discovering My Parents

i've been in Chicago now for well over a month. It just seems like I don't know what I'm doing at this time. I began working at a school and just taking one day at a time. My car is still in Cali at my aunt and uncle's house, and they are wondering when I'm coming back. I can't give them an answer. So, I keep praying they will stop asking me, to be honest. I would have liked to go and get my car, but my finances weren't there. It's just a lot, and I'm stressed out because I don't understand what is going on in my life. But guess what? I'm going with the flow and trying my hardest to trust God and not be so angry. I've found myself complaining and making excuses about every little thing but still forcing myself to keep moving forward. It's hard when you don't know what the next step is and you can hear from God. This is not an ideal statement, but I will be able to make sense of it as I continue to grow.

It's okay that I don't have all the answers for someone who thinks she knows it all a lot of times. LOL. It's not that He wasn't talking; I just wasn't listening and was wanting things to be done my way. We are all guilty of this very thing. I actually forgot what I prayed for. I asked God to allow me to get to know my mother like for real and be able to watch "Worst Cooks in America" with her. I felt like I didn't know her because of so many years of being away from her during undergrad, grad school and then moving to Cali. I was in a place in my life where I wanted to know my parents.

There are so many times where I would talk to my Mommie on the phone; and she would reflect so much on her memories with her mom, My Dear, which is what I called my grandmother. The love my mom had for her mom was deep, and mine wasn't as deep for my mom. I had an epiphany that our relationship was surface level. It had no depth, even though we had a decent relationship. There was just more out of the relationship that I wanted. So, I began to pray and ask God to show me how to grow my relationship with my mom the way that I envisioned it. I also began to ask God to change the things that I did not like about her, not in a sense that I wanted to change my mother. I knew that certain ways of thinking that she had would not form a healthier relationship between us because it would block our growth. And slowly but surely, I began to see changes.

I also started to work on my relationship with my father. I began to call him more and would ask questions about his father, my grandfather, and just getting more involved in his life. I think I owe that to myself and to my future children. Plus, I like history. And I came to find out that that was my daddy's favorite subject in high school as well. Let me brag on my dad for a bit. He was super talented, one of the best football players in his time. He wasn't a pro, but he could have been. His nickname was Breakaway. He was that fast. That explains why my twin brother could run so fast. My twin was superfast, and I was pretty fast as well. My father was in the Army and in the Vietnam War. He was a truck driver for many years, and he worked in construction. As a matter of fact, he helped build the Willis (Sears) Tower in Downtown Chicago. To say the least, my daddy is a cool dude in my book.

Yes, he left me and my twin when we were 2 years old. That hurt. But in all the pictures in the many photo albums that my mom has, he was there and active.

An interesting fact about me is that my twin and I were in pageants since birth. One time in a pageant, there was this segment where the parents had to compete to see who could put a diaper on their child/children the fastest. Of course, my daddy won that competition. Healthy competition has always been a trait in my bloodline. That explains the many talents and athleticism that flow through my little body. LOL. I love my parents, though they are flawed and dope as crap to me. I see why God had to put those two together to create little ol' me.

While on the phone with my father one day, he told me how they met. They both had friends that invited them to church. Yup, church. So, they went to church. And while at church, my mother caught my father's eye. Let's say things moved rather quickly, and the rest is history. So, that explains why I love God so much. He has always been there even before I was born. God is so dope, man!

My father's nickname back in the day and still to this day is Rev. Dr. Leroy because he is wise and is always educating others, and so am I. My mother's nickname is Sunshine because that is what she brings to any room she walks in. My Dear, my grandmother, gave her that name. That's my girl, hence why my name is Lenore, The Light. God knew what He was doing.

Outside of their relationship with God, a hobby or an interest that my parents shared was dancing. Those two on the dance floor are something else. So much joy radiates from their faces. I see where I get it from. I love dancing. I started dancing at the age of 3. Let's not get on how much of a jokester they are either. My mom cracks hecka jokes all day and so does my dad. He reminds me of my twin so much when I talk to him. They are men of a few words; but don't let them get to heating, flaming, roasting, cracking several jokes back-to-back on you. It's over with. LOL.

The moral of this piece of my book is that you have a choice to focus on the bad or hurtful parts of your parental relationships. The choice our parents made is what was the best decision in their minds for us at that time. Who are we to judge? All we can do is forgive and love. I'll choose the good in a person or situation any day.

Planning The 2nd Annual "Walk By Faith" Conference (2017)

Here we are again planning yet another conference. Initially, I knew that I would plan the conference every year unless God said otherwise. I was excited about the conference and how better it would be compared to last year's conference. I had high hopes since it would be held in Chicago for the second time. Last year, I was living in Los Angeles and planning the entire conference from another state. It wasn't that challenging at all. However, this year, I was looking for all types of venues in the city and in the suburbs. I was shocked on how quickly I secured my speakers. They both flew from L.A. to come and speak, even my praise dancer and another close friend of mine flew from there as well.

    We all were moving in faith, and it was beautiful. Mugs (people) were straight booking flights on faith. It was a movement. Throughout this time of planning, I wanted my speakers and myself fasting and participating in weekly prayer calls. They both were on board, and it was refreshing to talk to them each week and just pray as a unit. I am so glad to have had their support. I found myself creating yet another flyer on faith and posting it. I didn't have a venue or the funding, but I did what I knew I could do and that was to be obedient and take it day by day. I even asked a few of my students to volunteer to help with the welcome table on the day of the event. They were excited and eager to see how the event would turn out.

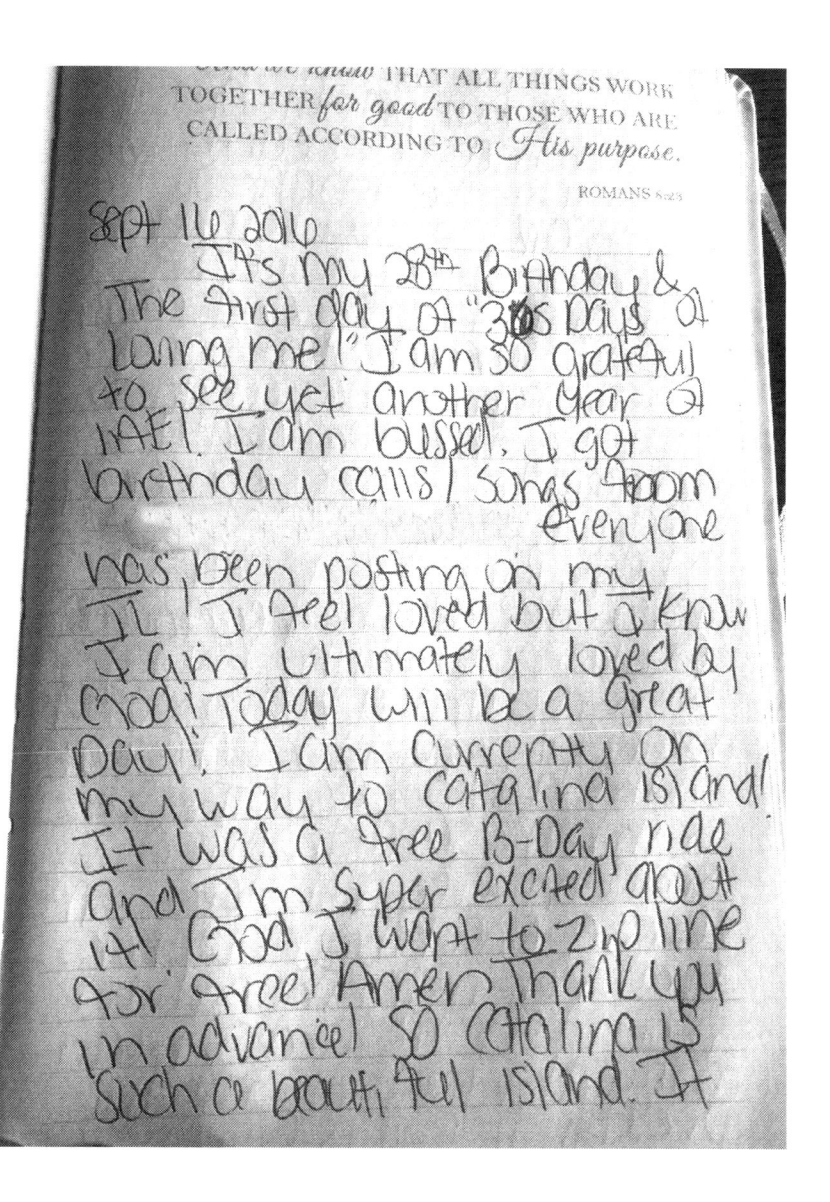

Chapter 7
365 Days Of Loving Me

> ...THAT ALL THINGS WORK TOGETHER *for good* TO THOSE WHO ARE CALLED ACCORDING TO *His purpose*.
> ROMANS 8:23

Sept 16, 2016

It's my 28th Birthday & the first day of "365 Days of Loving me!" I am so grateful to see yet another year of life! I am blessed. I got birthday calls/songs from everyone has been posting on my IL! I feel loved but I know I am ultimately loved by God! Today will be a great day!. I am currently on my way to Catalina Island! It was a free B-Day ride and I'm super excited about it. God I want to zip line for free! Amen Thank you in advance! So Catalina is such a beautiful island. It

*I*n September, on the day of my birthday, I decided to start blogging. I received so many prophecies about blogging during this time that I decided to just go with it. Choosing to be committed to blogging for roughly 52 weeks straight was a challenge. In some areas of my life, I battle with the spirit of procrastination and laziness. To others, it may not have seemed so because I was always doing something. I am a very outgoing person, and I love doing new things. I am adventurous. For me, the standard that I hold myself to is totally different than how others perceive me.

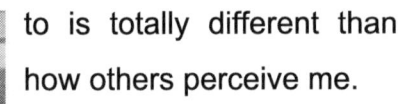

It's quite difficult to carry yourself at a lower expectation once you've seen or heard what God wants or has for you. Those visions and prophetic words are what I want to see manifest in my life. Nothing less. Some may even say I am too hard on myself, and that may be true to an extent; but I am just trying to live out the best version of myself. That's all.

My Birthday at Catalina Island

I am a person that is always self-evaluating and improving my thoughts and behaviors. What God thinks about me is a big deal; and I sometimes get in trouble with Him when I am overdoing it, but He gets me.

I chose to title my blog 365 DAYS OF LOVING ME, (https://brittanylenore.weebly.com/), because I wanted to love myself more. I wanted to learn to accept my flaws, and I wanted to overcome certain perceptions of myself. I wanted to become a young woman and be more mature. I also wanted to bare it all so that other women would become healed and set free from my honesty. Throughout the year, I struggled some weeks to post; but I did it. A good girlfriend of mine helped me edit my blogs, which was a blessing. My grammar wasn't the strongest at the time, but I continued to get better.

All Nations Worship Assembly – Chicago Campus

Worship at "The Well." Okay. So, let me just get this out now. I love me some Dr. Matthew L. Stevenson, III. Everyone has that one pastor that they just connect with their preaching and teachings. Well, he is that for me. When I hear him preach, teach, prophesy, it just amazes me how much he reminds me of myself, the version of myself now and my future self. He is such a leader, and I absolutely love his heart for God and God's people. I remember when I first heard him speak. It was at my old church, and I had never heard anyone in my adult life prophesy like him. He was so captivating and refreshing. I was blown away by just the sound of his voice and his accuracy. After that, I came across him on Periscope and have been hooked on his ministry ever since. He is just an amazing, raw, real and brilliant and funny human being whose heart is after Christ. I brag on him so much because I feel like his teachings are necessary and freeing. I have come out of so much bondage and false identity being under his teachings. Glory be to God!

In this time of living in Chicago, God allowed me to actually go to his church in the city. I remember living in Cali the first time and going to listen to him preach whenever he came to town. Look, wherever he is, I am trying to be there. It's that deep for me. I love his wife as well. She is such a beautiful person.

One Sunday, I am at his church and he is doing an altar call. I am sitting in my seat minding my business when, all of a sudden, the Holy Spirit said, "Get up." I'm like, "Who? Me?" I thought I was tweaking. LOL. So, I sat there. It's not like I didn't want to, but the instruction caught me off guard. So, by this being a prophetic church, two people randomly came up to me and said, "Don't miss your blessing." So, I'm just looking at them. So, he calls for the final altar call. And the Holy Spirit just lifts me out of my seat. Before you know it, I'm walking down the aisle; and I hear people saying, "That's Brittany." It was like I heard a crowd of people whispering. It was all eyes on me. Even Dr. Matthew L. Stevenson was staring at me.

In my head, I'm like, "No, Lord, don't have him lay hands on me. I'm not ready." I love the Lord and I desire to be taken under his anointing; but, at the same time, I was scared as crap. The Bible does say fear the Lord. So, I made it to the front and I felt fine. I was so happy to be an official member and a part of the "All Nations Worship Assembly," ANWA, family and under his covering.

I am going to touch on this really quickly, and then I'll think about coming back to it. I strongly, strongly dislike when people say who is your covering, meaning who is my pastor or spiritual mother/father. To me personally, I don't always have a direct human covering because I move around a lot. At one time, I did have a human covering; but that was only for a very short season, but not really. However, it is such a religious question to me; and it annoys me most of the time. My covering is the Holy Spirit, just like he was for Jesus.

> *The Bible says, "But the Comforter, even the Holy Spirit, whom the Father will send in my name, he shall teach you all things, and bring to your remembrance all that I said unto you," John 14:26 (ASV).*

People act like it's a sin to go without a covering. It's not my fault that God calls me to Himself and, in that time, I don't need no doggone covering because I have God Himself. I've asked God many times for a covering, and He said no. He specifically told me that He didn't want anyone taking advantage of my anointing at that time. I even asked Him to provide me with someone special in the right season of my life. I have learned to be okay with this. I know whose teaching I am submitted to.

Some people actually do need direct covering or they will backslide. God knows that, so He gives each person what they need. I actually prefer that you do have a covering, especially if you know that you could return to your old ways of sinful habits. I also do believe you need to find a church home that functions in the five-fold ministry: Apostles, prophets, evangelists, pastors and teachers. We will get into this a little later on in the book, maybe. With that being said, I want people to stop thinking that I need what they need. I don't. The Holy Spirit is my covering, and many will find this out sooner than later.

Chapter 8
Family Ties

family can be the toughest group of people to get along with. In all honesty, there was a time when certain perceptions of family were hidden. As a child, I think it was easier to see the good in anyone unless the person was just evil. Family members tend to make certain situations their business when it's simply not. We might come from the same bloodline; but in each family, there is a different set of rules in each home. That rule is you do what your momma and your daddy say regardless of what anyone else tells you to do. Would you rather get in trouble by your parents or a play family member? 'Cause back then and nowadays, everybody is your cousin. Stop it. LOL.

I remember one time while in high school, I had about six cousins going to my school. We were super deep. Let's just say we were all good-looking. And all my boy cousins, including my twin, were popular and known for throwing them hands. LOL.

I digress. Let's get back to the elements and characteristics of family members. We all have several types of individuals in our family. How about we go down the line: The BBQ thrower, the funny one, the drunk one, the smart one, the outcast, the creative, the alcoholic, the gay one, the one that only stays at get-togethers for five minutes, the fast one (hot in the pants), the one that has a different boyfriend or girlfriend at every get-together, the shy one, the liar, the storyteller, the one that takes all the pictures, the aunt or uncle that lets you get away with anything, the strict one, the nosey one, the mean one, the holy one, the dancer, the singer, the rapper, the entrepreneur, the hook-up, the selfish one, the giver, the one that cusses a lot, the traveler, the athlete, the thot. And the list goes on.

There are several family dynamics. Some are healthy, and some are very toxic. Either way, you didn't have an option to pick your family. So, what do you do? You learn how to deal with them, love them, support them and keep praying for them. I know, I know. Some people reading this will say, "I ain't praying for none of them. I don't even talk to them." I know. I've been there and felt probably every emotion that most people feel when it comes to the disappointments and the celebratory moments of family members.

Here, let me tell you a story. I was staying back in Chicago with my mom. This is when I moved back home unexpectedly from L.A. and was subbing at the schools. I had been home for some time; and I had seen several things with my mom's living arrangements that I was just not in agreement with, neither was she. She didn't want to say it, but I could feel it. It was almost as if she thought she was stuck. This very story is why I think the Lord brought me home when He did. There is a season for everything, and there is a time in the earth when cycles have to come to an end.

So, there was a discrepancy between my aunt and myself. From her perspective, I was confused and trying to find myself, which wasn't the case at all. I was honestly sure about myself and why God brought me back home and the point I was at in my life. Her comment regarding my life at that time did try to plant itself as a seed in my life. But thank God for the Holy Spirit who constantly reassured me of who I was.

I came to the conclusion that the evil spirits that were in the building did not like that I was there. They hated that my spirit was there and was challenging the routine of things that should have never been. When the Bible talks about your spirit having the ability to shift atmospheres, it's real.

> *1 Samuel 16:23 says, "And it came to pass, when the evil spirit from God was upon Saul, that David took an harp, and played with his hand: So Saul was refreshed, and was well, and the evil spirit departed from him" (KJV).*
>
> *1 Kings 8:10-11 says, "When the priests withdrew from the Holy Place, the cloud filled the temple of the LORD. And the priests could not perform their service because of the cloud, for the glory of the LORD filled his temple" (NIV).*

You are the light. Your role as a kingdom kid is to expose darkness and the evil works of Satan and his "fake" army. I don't like the dude at all, and you will be able to tell better later on in this book.

Anywho, I saw through the manipulation, the bitterness, the jealousy and the control operating in the household in general. I actually hate the spirit of control. It is one of the worst evil spirits a person can operate in directly in front of me.

So, let me set the scene from my point of view. I can only tell my side of the story because this is my book. Also, it wouldn't be fair to give too much detail without the consent of my aunt. Okay. So one day, my mom was in the kitchen. For some reason, my aunt was downstairs in our apartment. My mom and I are super close. My mom is not perfect by far at all. And she has a mouth on her, not like she used to; but my mom is sweet. Sometimes she can choose not to vocalize herself when she really needs to. She can go from a pit bull with her words to a little toddler with her level of sensitivity. These are the characteristics we share, but now I use mine the right way. I've learned how to shift my tone and alter my word choices when necessary.

I forget how the argument started. It's really a blur right now; but I just know my aunt and I were going toe-to-toe, no cursing, which I am proud about. But I snapped on her, like I was going in and just really saying some true stuff, just not in a loving way. Once I felt my mom holding me back, I knew that I personally had went too far. I had never argued with an adult like that in my life. My mom didn't raise me that way at all. I transformed right before my very eyes. Don't get me wrong. I have cursed some folks clean out, but never an adult.

When I felt my mom's hand holding me back, I realized that she was standing in between us. I came to. It was like I was watching the situation outside of my own body while it was happening. It was almost as if God pulled me out of myself to see the entire situation for what it was. Then I heard the Lord say, "It's the spirit of anger." As soon as I heard that, I said it and I rebuked the spirit. I looked my aunt dead in her face and said, "I rebuke you, spirit of anger."

Now I could see with my spiritual eyes with the mind of God. The spirit of anger tried to speak some words after but couldn't. I walked away and went into the bathroom. I was so angry with myself. I began to ask God how could I go that far. I was so mad that I was going to fight my aunt. It would have turned ugly because the whole family would have been involved then, and that wasn't even the intention.

I was and had been at a place in my life where I was a loner. No one understood me, as it seemed, especially my family. My Mommie had patience with me because I was her child, and I know this for a fact. All I wanted was for the devil to stop wreaking havoc in my life and in my family's life. The devil has tried to destroy my family for so long by bringing division, confusion, lies, mistrust and even perversion. I felt like I was the only one that could see it. And now since I had a new set of eyes, I was the target. My relationships have been sabotaged by the enemy, and my intentions in many of my relationships dealing with friends and ex-boyfriends have been misrepresented because of his craftiness.

I hate the devil! He will use old tricks to stir your emotions in the very thing that God pulled you out of. If you don't constantly seek God in the areas where you struggle, the enemy will try to devour you.

> *The Bible says in 1 Peter 5:8-9, "Be alert and of sober mind. Your enemy the devil prowls around like a roaring lion looking for someone to devour. Resist him, standing firm in the faith, because you know that the family of believers throughout the world is undergoing the same kind of sufferings" (NIV).*

I asked God for forgiveness. I never apologized to my aunt still to this day. I have seen her, but I didn't feel that she was open to me speaking to her. I plan to fix this real soon. Sometimes with family, you have to look past the natural and deal with the core of a person and see them the way God sees them. I am not saying don't use discernment or protect your heart and feelings. I am saying that there is a time in your life where you will have to allow your emotions about a situation or a person to die in order to see the salvation of the Lord in your bloodline.

I am not perfect, but I strive every day to be a better person. The devil can't have my family! I stay on my face for them, and I choose to be bold in my love for Christ in the hopes that this will draw my family to true salvation and deliverance. The change has to start with you first. Many of us are looked over and counted out, but we are the ones God is going to use to pull the ones close to us out of darkness. So, if this is you, just decree this now:

"Because I am saved and serve the Lord Jesus with my whole heart, my family is saved! I am the forerunner of my family,

*and I carry the spirit of deliverance to break generational curses in my bloodline in **Jesus' name!**"* Brittany Lenore.

The things that I battle are not because I am doing something wrong; it's because I am fighting a battle for my family. I am constantly fighting the demons that they wrestle with. If you are chasing after Jesus and you feel like the attacks are coming back-to-back, KEEP MOVING! If there's no pressure, then that means you are on the wrong team. Keep fighting, keep fasting, keep praying, keep overcoming. Don't give up. God will send the ravens to feed you like he did Elijah when Jezebel was after him and trying to kill him. He will give you what you need to endure through the battle, the offense, the betrayal, the lies and the loneliness. If I can get through it, so can you. You are a warrior, and you are a winner. Our Father in Heaven is VICTORIOUS!

Chapter 9
Supernatural Publishing

I never understand how the Lord will move. It was such a challenge for me to push my first *Blind Faith* book out. Now I am here writing my third book, which is the sequel to the first one I wrote. Who would have thought it? It's funny how you can never imagine certain things for your life until you allow God to direct your path. Allowing God to get in the driver's seat makes life easier and clearer because He can see far up ahead.

Things that we struggle to see when we are driving, He sees. He is the best driver in the worst conditions of our life, conditions such as emotional struggles like anxiety, depression, low self-esteem, mood swings and anxiousness. These conditions represent rain, snow, fog, smoke, all the things that would be challenging for us to see while driving. The best thing about this is that God can command anything that is clouding our judgment to be removed from us, and this is what the hand of God in your life should look like on a daily basis. He is the author and finisher of your story. I say this to say He literally guided my hands to do the unthinkable, which is to tell the world the most vulnerable parts of me and not be bound by guilt or shame.

Instead, he healed, delivered and gave me a fresh identity into who I was and could be. Not everyone is meant to be an author; but everyone is responsible for telling their story, whether that be in a documentary, a film, a painting, speaking engagements, music or sports. Your expression of your story is what makes you unique. I encourage you to really encourage yourself to move in confidence and know that your story matters and can impact the lives of many.

It will be a challenge to get your message out to the world because the enemy doesn't want you to tell it. But just keep going. You can do it. I have stopped and started writing my book so many times that it's not even funny. But that something, being the Holy Spirit, deep down on the inside of me is what allows me to birth every possible thing inside of me. God has His hand on your destiny, and nothing can stand in the way of what He wants to do but you. So, my advice to you would be to start again.

Moving back to Chicago wasn't a curse but a blessing. I soon found out why I needed to come back. My help was here. As I researched how to publish a book, I just began to become overwhelmed. I was worried about the wrong thing before even finishing what God told me to do. The instruction was to simply "Write the book." I was doing too much. Don't we all do that? Like, we are already thinking 30 steps ahead without even finishing the first step. LOL. Jeez.

In the moments where I became frustrated, I would hear the voice of the Lord saying "Finish the book" or "Write the book." He literally wouldn't say anything else. So, one day I reconnected with a childhood friend of mine who lived across the street from me when we were kids. I forget how we even reconnected, but God allowed us to cross paths. FYI: I never remember my first encounters with others, but somehow they always remember how they encountered me. LOL. Yet, it is always some dramatic experience. It never fails.

Anywho, we began to catch up and talk about God; and she began to express to me what she had been asking God to do in her. She asked Him to allow her to be able to help His people with what she has on the inside of her. I asked her what is that? What did she want to do? I knew that she was artistic. Since we were young, she could draw really well. So, I assumed that's what she was speaking of, which, in a sense, it was. I dug deeper. I ask a lot of questions anyway. I'm, low-key, a little nosey but not in a bad way. LOL. I just have a gift to pull information out of people gracefully. She expressed that her career path was formatting and publishing books for a living. She even published books for many well-known and credible people. Never in a million years would I have suspected that she would say this and that God would provide me with a direct resource like that.

It was never about the HOW. It was always about the INSTRUCTION. Jesus! God just wants you to DO WHAT HE TELLS YOU TO DO. Hallelujah! Don't ask any questions. Just be obedient with the one thing He has told you to do. Once you can get past that step, then the next will come. We can get so caught up on worrying about how things are going to get done that we miss out on the blessings by trying to move ahead of God. No. Be still, sons and daughters of God. God has you, and help is on the way.

> *The Bible says, "Be still, and know that I am God" Psalms 46:10 (NIV).*

If you are reading this, YES, I am talking to you. Where God leads and/or instructs, He provides. There is provision in the assignment for you, and there are Heavenly resources. God has ordained relationships set up just for you if you will only trust Him.

My childhood friend and I began to discuss in more detail about what I needed to do to get this book finished. I really appreciated her help and her mom's help. She and her mom helped me edit the book and gave me great advice on how to structure my thoughts and sentences. I so needed this. My childhood friend walked me through the entire process and still helps me to this day. I took what I learned and wrote my second book, *Prophetic Phrases*, which is a book of poems. Writing is time-consuming, but it's worth it once you read the testimonies that are attached to your obedience and discipline. If God has appointed you to be a scribe, a songwriter, a poet, a transcriber, a journalist, etc., *I decree that your gift will bless you and be used to advance the Kingdom of God, in Jesus' name!*

Chapter 10
Hearing God During Transitions

*I*n this chapter, I will briefly discuss the importance of hearing God in the process of a transition. This is very critical because this is when the enemy likes to come and try to confuse and disrupt the works of the Lord. In God, there is always an appointed time, whether we would like to believe it or not. When God is ready to move in your life, He always prepares your heart. That's No. 1.

No. 2. He sends confirming words in whichever way He needs to get the message across. He may speak to you through different vessels or outlets (the Bible, magazines, conversations, text messages, music, TV shows, etc.). God will use ANYTHING to get your attention.

No. 3. He will send you help. This may be a family member, a friend, a neighbor, a co-worker or a brother or sister in Christ who is a complete stranger. They may come offering the solution to what you may be questioning God about or subconsciously worried about. In this, you will have to simply trust God. Don't think too hard on it. And remember what you asked God for.

A true indicator in your transition or decision that it is truly a God thing is that it's EASY, so easy that your mind can't even fathom how all things are working in your favor. God loves to do this kind of stuff. He gets joy watching you go through the process of trusting Him and receiving that very thing you believed Him for, even if you doubted it a few times in the process. He knows your heart and your ways. Relax and say YES to His will and His way!

My mom had been through a rough time while I was living with her. I saw a lot, and I prayed a lot about the things that I could not verbally address because it wasn't my place to. For me, I stayed encouraging my mom and she encouraged me too. I feel as if every time I had real breaking moments in my life, God has always made sure I was in the comfort of my mother's arms. It's like I've legit been through hell and back. And somehow when I am at my breaking point, God makes sure my mom is there to impart her faith, love and encouragement to me.

That's so POWERFUL, you guys.

Now, my mom expressed to me that her lease was up and she is ready to move. I was in full support. She wanted a change, and she said that she felt as if the Lord was giving her permission to leave and go where He was leading her. My mom is a prophetic dreamer. That is one of her gifts. Those of you who dream often, begin to write your dreams down or voice record them, whether they are good or bad. The Lord is trying to communicate with you in such a beautiful way. In the Bible, Nebuchadnezzar was a dreamer. And Daniel could interpret visions and dreams. When you get a chance, read the Book of Daniel. I wasn't really a dreamer myself until I asked God for this gift, then He just awakened what was inside of me because I asked.

So, it's now moving day. I literally packed my mom's whole house up. It was an extremely hard task, and I was annoyed with my mom because she can be a bit impulsive with her decision-making. I am a huge thinker. So, when something is not thought out thoroughly and it doesn't make sense, I become upset, especially if I know for a fact it could have been handled better and more efficiently.

Either way, at this point, I couldn't do anything about it but suck it up and hurry up and get on the road. So, we are finally on the road and well over halfway there. My mom expresses to me that the leasing agency just quoted her a higher price for the apartment from the original amount. Look, my mom had just enough money to move in. She was so upset and so was I because we just packed up and left everything. There was no going back. Mind you, I was driving her car; and she was driving the U-Haul truck. So, I just began to pray and to call out to God to help us. I was weeping, y'all, 'cause I knew what time it was. The devil thought he was being slick. I began to pray in tongues, and I turned on my worship music.

In the midst of all that I was doing, God projected a vision onto my mind. It was as if I was seeing it with my natural eyes. But clearly, I was driving. I am a seer. This means that God reveals prophetic revelations to my spirit which is projected onto my mind in present time. However, when operating in this gift, God can show a person images, conversations, places, people, etc., from the past, present and/or future. This ability is commonly known as déjà vu; but it is not and not common, might I add.

The ability to operate in this gift is much more tested and proved by God in order to become more accurate, detailed and familiar with what He is trying to show you. The vision that I saw was a newly-remodeled apartment with white walls and light wood floors and cabinets. I quickly realized that this was God speaking to me. He was assuring me of the very thing that we were believing for was already set in our favor. The Lord is Jehovah-Jireh, the God that provides.

I called my mother and told her what I saw, and I also told her to have faith. Apparently, there was only one apartment available; and that was the one we were misquoted for. We arrived at the new destination, and the leasing manager is there waiting to show us the apartment.

Now, we entered into one apartment. It was cool, but that apartment wasn't it. My mom liked it; but I was like, "Nah, ma, this doesn't match my vision." So, I asked the man, "Are there any more apartments available?" He said, "Yes, but they won't be ready until a few days from now; but I can show them to you."

This situation reminds me of the story of David in the Bible when Samuel asked David's father Jesse do you have another son? See, David wasn't prepared to meet Samuel, nor was he ever intended to be considered as an option. Just like Samuel, I asked the leasing agent were there any more apartments. They weren't necessarily ready to be shown, but I was able to view them just by asking.

My mom was annoyed, tired, hot and was willing to settle. Not me. My faith was focused on what God showed me. He is not a man that He should lie.

The leasing agent showed us the second apartment, and my Spirit Man said the same thing: "Not this one." The very last apartment was located in the back corner of all the other apartment complexes. We walked up the stairs to the apartment. He opens the door. And what do I see? A newly-remodeled apartment with white walls and light wooden floors. I said, "Mommie, this is it, the apartment from my vision." The only thing that was missing from the apartment was the stove, which they brought on that following Monday.

My mom had never seen me operate in my gifts like that as an adult. There was one time as a child that she saw me operate in my gifts. I am so glad that she trusted the God in me that day. I was so humbled and glad that

I was with her on this journey. I may even write a book on this gift more in-depth in the future when I learn more about it.

Chapter 11
The Benefits of Corporate Prayer & Fasting

R.I.P Ms. Denise

*a*s I am rapidly preparing for the "Walk By Faith" conference, the Holy Spirit lead me to call a corporate fast with all the speakers and the dancer. I never really asked anyone to fast with me before. The first year, it was just myself and a friend who volunteered to help. So, I knew that when it was time to fast, I was always serious about it and never broke a fast. I feel like fasting is a huge commitment not only to God but to yourself. Fasting, to me, shows how serious you are about your relationship with God. When I fast, I mentally prepare myself. I don't care if I am fasting for 3 or 40 days, which I have done both on several occasions, I have to prepare my heart, mind and spirit. If I don't, then I may fail. And in my mind, I can't let God down. I can't speak for all people that fast, but this is my mentality going into it.

When God called us to fast, literally everybody jumped on board. We were all operating in faith and believing God to do mighty things in us and through us.

> *2 Timothy 2:21 says, "If you keep yourself pure, you will be a special utensil for honorable use. Your life will be clean, and you will be ready for the Master to use you for every good work." (NLT).*

I mean as we prepared for the conference, we all pressed to the throne room and just really covered every area in prayer. At this time, we still did not have a venue; but the flyer was published and we had people registered already. Even the speakers by this time had already booked their tickets in faith.

Chapter 12
I Got Shot At! Real Bullets

*t*he title of this chapter is already mind-blowing, I know. So, take a deep breath with me and let's travel back down this road. You are probably wondering, Brittany, how in the heck did you find yourself in this situation? Would you believe that I actually saw the shooting happen in a vision moments before it happened? I was in the house one night, and one of my good girlfriend's brother had a friend and that friend wanted to hang out with me. I was debating if I wanted to go or not. So, of course I asked God; and He was cool with it. Let me tell y'all God is not the man you think that He is. He is super dope and chill. LOL. Then I told one of my other friends at the time about it, and she said she didn't get a bad feeling about it.

Y'all, I wasn't really trying to go on dates for real. He texted me and told me we were going to go downtown with one of his cousins. That was cool because I didn't want to go anywhere else. He was about 6'3" with a nice chocolate complexion and had a gorgeous smile and perfect teeth. He was a little younger than me, but it was all good because it was innocent. He asked to take me out, not to date me. Relax, guys. LOL.

So, he picked me up from my home. But as we were walking to the car, I saw another dude in the car. I asked him who was that. He said, "Oh, that's my cousin's friend. I didn't know he was coming with us. My cousin picked me up, and he was in the car." I expressed to him that I didn't want to be riding in the car with a whole bunch of dudes. That doesn't look good that I'm the only female in the car. I just wasn't raised like that. He said, "Don't worry about him. You're gonna be with me once we get downtown." I said, "Okay, but it's something about dude that ain't right."

So, his cousin was driving. But then we started going the other direction. I'm like, "Wait. This ain't the way to go downtown." His cousin was like we gonna stop in this suburb, a suburb that I knew was known for not being a good area. I said, "Ain't nothing good about that particular suburb but trouble." I told him that I didn't want to go there. This is why I hate riding with other people for this very reason.

We pulled up to some bar, and the people hanging

outside the bar just looked super hood and ratchet. Ugh! I told the guy I was with that I didn't want to go in there and that I'll wait outside. He was like, "Come on, man. You're with me. I don't want to be here either." I rolled my eyes super hard. We go in. And when I tell y'all the spot was so tiny, it was really tiny. It looked like a hallway. No lie. I was pissed off. I sat down instantly and peeped (scouted) the scene out. I knew no one. That was another sign right there, a red flag right there. I ain't never been that close to home where I didn't know anyone. Yo, anywhere I go, I know somebody. Ask any of my friends.

We sat down and were flirting a little bit. And then, all of a sudden, I feel eyes on me, like, ladies, you know when other females are staring hard as crap, plotting and hating. I'm like, yo, I'm too old for this. So, there was this group of little ugly, young females just eyeballing us. I asked him like, "Do you know them?" He said, "I only know one of them, but not like that."

So, I walked to the bathroom; and they all walked behind me. So, I let them get in front of me because what you ain't gonna do is catch me off guard or from behind. They all go into a one-stall bathroom. Y'all know how that goes. So, I'm waiting outside; and I let another young lady go before me because she had to go really bad. The group of girls were in there for a minute. So, the young lady started to bang on the door for them to hurry up. In the midst of that, the young lady decides that she can't hold it. So, she leaves the bar to go use it outside. LOL.

So, they finally came out and were looking at me and mean-mugging me as if I banged on the door. In my head, I'm like let one of these h**s swing; I'll just be fighting for my life period. They didn't say anything, though. They just kept walking.

While in the bathroom, I'm praying and telling God like I can just go sit in the car. I was so over it. By the time I got back to the guy I came with, he's smiling at me extra hard. And then he says, "You want to go sit in the car?" I'm like, "Yup. You read my mind." We get to the car, and we're listening to music and talking for about a good five to eight minutes. All of a sudden, I get a vision of them shooting outside the bar. So, I vocalized to him what I saw. I didn't know what his belief was, and I didn't care. So, as he was calling his cousin to tell him to come on, his cousin was walking across the parking lot. He gets in the car, and the cousin's friend was missing. Then dude's cousin said, "I'll call him and tell him to come out."

So, while this is happening, everyone is coming out of the bar. The scene in front of me started to look like my vision. I'm like, "Yo, let's go. Something doesn't feel right." Of course, this little dummy is arguing with someone; and the cousin is telling him to come on. Y'all, why in the hell did this dummy take somebody's gun off their lap while they were sitting on a dirt bike? Like how did he possibly think that was gonna fly?

So, me and the dude I was with were like leave him. "Let's go!" We were legit screaming at his cousin while the cousin is telling his little dumb friend to get in the car. We are screaming from the back seat, "HELL, NAH. DON'T LET HIM IN THIS CAR! DRIVE!" So now I'm like "f" this. I'm grabbing for the door handle to get out, and I couldn't. It was locked. I was panicking. Then I heard, "He's got a gun! Duck!" The guy I was with covered me on the back seat, and all I heard were rapid gunshots and that the car was still not moving. Bullets were flying through the windows of the car, and then the car starting moving and driving superfast. They were still shooting.

I was screaming "JESUS, HELP US! HELP US,

JESUS!" It seemed as if the people that were shooting at us were driving alongside of us. The guy I was with started yelling, "I think I'm shot!" I was scared to look up, but I knew my surroundings and was giving directions to the nearest hospital. We didn't even make it to the hospital before we were stopped by the police. I was praying. They had a big open bottle of Hennessy in the car and a loaded unregistered gun. I'm like, "Yo, I ain't going to jail for NOBODY."

This next part that I'm about to express was nothing but GOD even more so. We got out of the car, and there were about five police cars. I was checking dude's body to make sure he wasn't shot. He was just in shock because some glass had shattered on top of him, but he was okay. We were standing on the sidewalk, and he was checking me to make sure I was okay and saying how sorry he was for putting me in this situation. In the meantime, the police started checking the whole car. I was so nervous that they were going to find all that illegal stuff. I mean they were looking all throughout the car, and we are standing by watching them. The police didn't find anything. I don't know how, but all I can say is, "But God!"

So, I was calling an Uber to leave by this time because I was not getting back in that car. An officer came over to us and asked basic questions. After he was done, we started to walk away. The officer said, "Where are you guys going?" I said, "Home." He smirked and said, "You can't go home yet. We are in the middle of an investigation." I said, "Oh." Can y'all tell I don't know anything about being in trouble with the law? I sat on the curb until we were released.

Little dummy left with his friends, and we went with the cousin. We switched cars. And then me and ol' boy went to a hotel. We got a room because we didn't want to go home after that. It was hecka late, and we were shaken up. So, we held each other for most of the night. I say most of the night 'cause your girl was on the toilet. My nerves were shot, and I couldn't control myself. LOL. He didn't care that I spent most of my time on the toilet. We took turns sleeping, the little that we could. We comforted each other during the startling moments of being in shock, randomly waking up out of our sleep thinking that the shooting was occurring all over again.

What a night! I told only two people about this at that time. I didn't tell my mom at all because I just didn't want her worrying about me. She does that enough. That would have just sent her over the edge. I didn't tell people until the "Walk By Faith" Conference. I released it as a fresh testimony and described my reproach of the enemy and how God protected my life. I knew not to tell my mom when it happened for many reasons. When my mom heard me share this testimony at the conference, she almost fainted. She couldn't believe her ears. YIKES!

Chapter 13
Another FREE Venue Space

Whoa! I know that the last chapter was pretty intense, guys. But, hey, I'm alive, blessed and covered by the Blood. So, here I am still looking for a free venue. I've been calling all types of folks and places and kept getting roadblocks. You would think that I would have had more support with planning and securing a place by me being at home, but nope. I don't let adversity stop me at all. For some odd reason, I have learned how to persevere with mighty strength. God has allowed me to soar in the most adverse situations that were meant to destroy parts of me. He said, "No. My daughter shall live and not die." Satan has no authority over your life unless you give him power and access to it. He is super weak and don't you ever forget that.

> *Luke 10:19 says, "I have given you authority to trample on snakes and scorpions and to overcome all the power of the enemy; nothing will harm you" (NIV).*

Another FREE Venue Space

It is now two weeks before the conference and still no venue. I was working at a high school at the time, and there was a church right across the street. I felt led to stop by after work a few times but never did. However, on this one particular day, I chose to call the church. I spoke with an older man and told him what I wanted to do with the space. He told me to come by and check it out and that I could have the space. Yo, I was so excited but beating myself up at the same time. I say this because I should have listened a long time ago to the promptings of the Holy Spirit to reach out to that church. I would have saved myself a lot of time. But the greatest thing about God is that He will wait for you. No matter how long it takes for you to get it, He will wait; and what is meant for you will be for you. He is just that type of God. I love that Man! Glory! God may delay, but He never disappoints. WOW. My mind is blown even as I type these words. So, I go and visit the venue; and it's perfect. It was an upgrade from the last place; and it had a kitchen this time, y'all. Hallelujah!

Chapter 14
The 2nd Annual Walk By Faith Conference (2017)

*n*ow it's just days before the conference, and my speakers and dancer are flying in. Everything is falling into place, and I even had some little helpers. A few of my students offered to volunteer to set up, decorate and work the sign-in table, which was so sweet of them. My college mentor/big sister was my photographer and videographer. Praise God. We received monetary donations that helped out with the food and the love offering to give to the church. They didn't request it, but I offered it to the church because of my gratitude for them allowing me to have the space.

Up until the last minute, I had a few people registering. These were people that I would least have expected to register for the conference, but I was so happy. I just wanted to be obedient and do the work of the Lord. That's all I really cared about. I'm always in a state of expectancy for His Glory to fall when I do stuff like this.

When I say His Glory, I mean the supernatural, like signs, healings, miracles, breakthroughs, deliverance, prophecies, anything out of the daily norm.

It's finally the big day. My speakers, friends and the dancer are all here; and everybody had supernatural provisions for getting to Chicago for the conference because they operated in faith. It is a FAITH conference, right? Every time before a conference, I am super anxious to see what God will do. I just want to see the Heavens open up and the Glory of the Lord lifted on high. I'm just really a person that lives more in the supernatural than the natural. Most times, people encourage me and remind me that I am human. I know this but I just don't like to disappoint God, if I can help it. His approval of my life is all I want and need. He is my Savior and my greatest gift. Without Him, I am nothing; and I will never stop emptying myself out at His feet.

> *2 Corinthians 5:7 is my favorite scripture. It says, "For we walk by faith, not by sight" (NKJV).*

So, I rest in His presence and become reassured that whoever will attend the conference will be the ones who need to be there, even if it's one person. God goes after that one person and leaves the 99 because He cares that much. Also, that one person after God's heart and agenda can save a nation. I prefer to be the one that He calls so I can reach the 99. This life that He has called me to is so beautiful. I love Him so much and couldn't have imagined this life for myself; and it has just begun! I plan to continue to write and share my love for Him with the world. I am unashamed and unshackled. I am never going back.

As I pray and stay in expectation for my guests to arrive, I am filled with joy. I mean people traveled from all over to come, individuals that I have known since I was a child, even from my college days and even people that I poured into when I hosted Bible studies for small groups. God is faithful, and it matters that much when you love people and only want the best for them and then you see the fruits of your labor manifest. You guys, we worshipped, prayed and wept before God. It was such a beautiful sight to see.

Chapter 15
God Called Me To Entrepreneurship

As you know, as of 2017, I'm back in the Chicagoland area and living with my mom in a one-bedroom apartment. I'm just glad my mom always has a couch for me. Heck, she saw how uncomfortable I was and went and bought a let-out couch for me. I was thirsty that day. But those of you who don't know me, I'll make a pallet any day and sit on the floor Indian style before I sit in a chair. It's where I'm most comfortable, to be honest.

So, I was thinking and meditating on what I should do next. I'm like, "God, why am I here?" Still, no one would hire me. I was getting frustrated and getting up in age; and I had nothing, in my eyes, to show for my hard work. I pressed into God and fasted and waited for Him to reveal the answer to me. I started attending this prophetic church, and I would just go to church and meet God. I mean going to this church blessed me and strengthened my relationship even more with Christ. Sometimes, you don't need anything but a touch from

Him and He makes it all better.

One night, I decided to write my goals down and put them on the wall behind the front door. The Sticky Notes were all color-coordinated. I'm like my momma is gonna be like, "Brittany, what in the hell?" LOL. But I needed to see my goals and reference them every day. I am a planner; and I always write three months of goals in maybe five categories. That helps me way more than writing yearly goals, even though I write those as well. With the life I live, plans can change in a blink of an eye because I am led by the Spirit of God. And I love that actually. I guess I will tell you all my strategies. LOL.

So, for example, my categories would be: The Lenore, Inc.; Personal Development; Lenore The Light Ministry; Books; Spiritual Development and Social Media, among some others. Then I would put maybe three to five bullet points of goals under each category for the next three months. The things that I do complete, I put the date that it manifested next to it. After that, whatever I don't complete, I move to the next set of months. It's that simple. You are welcome, guys.

I even wrote affirmations and stuck them on the door to help me through such a trying season. I was tired, y'all. I would yell at the top of my lungs like, "God, do you see me? I'M TIRED!" I cried so many nights and would call my friends and weep and just vent. They let me vent. They encouraged me, prayed for me, loved me, cursed me out and decreed the blessings of the Lord over me. It was beautiful. It prepared me for the things that I could not see and still can't, but I truly trust God's timing and God's plan for me.

After I wrote my plans and was talking to a really good friend at the time and helping her with her business, I decided to move forward with my own. I learned so much from her at the time about business. I mean whenever we talked on the phone, the creative juices would just flow. It was so organic, pure and motivating. She literally had the language that I needed for what I wanted to do. I was the strategy person for both of our companies. I was planning and helping to implement and revamp business plans way before I had my own company. That blew my mind, but it was so fun.

So, I remembered the conversations that I had with my brothers regarding the name of my company. I was advised by my friend to Google the name to see if anyone else had it. They did. I was salty. LOL. But I just decided to put the word "The" in front of it. My oldest brother came up with The Lenore Group, and my twin said just call it Lenore Consulting. I mixed the two and got The Lenore, Inc.

I was then advised by my friend to get an EIN number, which anyone desiring to start a business should do. This can easily be done through the IRS website for free. Don't get nervous, guys. I know when you hear the initials IRS, most people get nervous. LOL. But the website is a good resource for business. But the proper order to start a business is by deciding what type of business you want first. If possible, talk it over with a certified public accountant (CPA). This person will help you decide whether your business should be an LLC, LLP, S Corp, sole proprietorship, etc. After that, then you can register for an EIN.

So, the summer of 2014, the idea of becoming a business owner was stirred up in my spirit. Then in November of 2017, my company was officially created.

On January 1, 2018, my company was birthed and launched. I have had entrepreneurial skill sets since forever. God always leaves pieces of your identity in plain sight so that you will always find your way back to His original intent for your life.

Chapter 16
A Starbucks Barista. Oh, Lord!

*b*arista. Who would have thought that I would be working at Starbucks? I was in a place where I was applying for state jobs, taking tests, applying online and still nothing. I'm like, "Lord, do you want me to work a minimum wage job or what?" That sounded so crazy to me, for real. So, I humbled myself and started applying for holiday positions to places like Bath & Body Works, temp agencies and other places. I don't actually remember how this came about. However, I do remember my sister in Christ, Kay, texted me and told me she had a vision of me in a green apron. I was like, "Ah, nah, Jesus. Starbucks?" I did not want to work there. I didn't know anything about coffee, bruh; and I wasn't feeling any of it. I just couldn't understand the reason behind all of it.

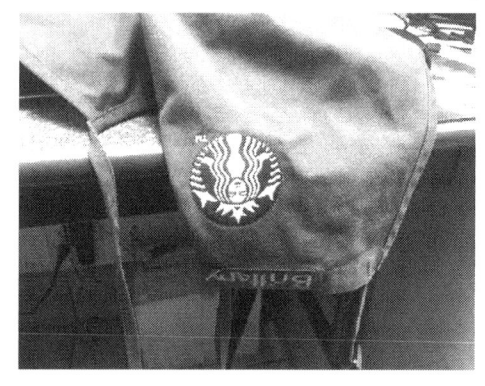

I was so depressed. I hated the thought of settling. I wasn't thinking about doing what I had to do until I could do better. That mentality was far from my mind because I felt like I was working crappy jobs already. It sucked, and I was pissed. I legit was mad. This is how uninterested I was about the whole idea: I rebuked Kay, LOL, as if any other time she texted me she wasn't prophetically on point. Ha-ha-ha! I wasn't going, y'all, I promise. But I said, "Okay, God. If I apply to this company and they are the first ones to call me back for an interview, I'll do it."

As I lay across my mother's bed with the laptop in front of me, I filled out the application, typing angrily with one finger. I submitted the application and thought to myself, Brittany, everything God asks you to do won't always be something you want to do. But will you still say Yes? Yo, the thought of this statement really had me questioning my Yes, especially since I was faced with all these mixed emotions and unanswered questions. The one thing I wasn't was confused. Even though I didn't have all the answers, I knew that God was with me and that I was doing exactly what He wanted me to do. I won't doubt God, and I fought very hard in this season of my life for my faith in Him.

It's the next day and I'm minding my own business, okay? I get a phone call from the store manager at Starbucks asking me to come in for an interview. I was so doggone mad and semi-happy all at the same time. I was mad because I didn't want to work there and that Kay was right. LOL. I was happy because I finally got an interview after so many months. I had to text my sister in Christ and tell her to keep using her gift, even when people rejected it. LOL. I was being petty; and I was in my feelings, high-key. I went to the interview and killed it, of course. They gave me my apron and schedule, and I worked there for six months before I moved back to L.A. I secured the Starbucks job in December. And around February or March, I wanted to quit. I asked God when will I go back to Cali.

Pause. So, when I got hired, my good Nigerian male friend bought me a bus pass with 20 rides on it. At this point, I may have used about 10 rides. They were hole-punched by the bus driver. Let's fast forward back to me asking God when will I go back to Cali. The Lord said, "When your bus pass runs out." I'm thinking like okay, Jesus, that's going to be real soon. Noooo. If I could

A Starbucks Barista. Oh, Lord!

insert an emoji here, I would.

    Y'all, I had favor with my bus driver. Every time I rode with this one driver, because my work schedule was basically the same every day, ugh, he would never punch a new hole on my bus card. LOL. He would punch the same one. The only time my bus card would get punched in a different spot was if I rode a different bus, which only happened like three times. God knew exactly what He was doing, and the bus driver submitted to what the Lord wanted for me. He probably doesn't even know why he kept feeling the urge to punch the same hole on the bus card. Long story short, I rode on that same bus pass for six months; and I was only initially supposed to have 20 rides on that bus card. CRAZY. LOL.

Overall, my experience at Starbucks was cool. They are one of the only companies that provided full benefits for part-time workers. They also have a partnership with a university that if you wanted to further your education, they would pay for that as well. I loved getting free pastries and free drinks. Now I'm addicted to the place.

They also had this program called the "Cup Fund." This program allows employees to donate any monetary amount of their paycheck to this fund. The fund is to help support employees and their families during natural disasters, which is super dope.

Lastly, while working there, I had an opportunity to go and volunteer with an organization called All Hands and Hearts (AHAH). This opportunity did not come through Starbucks. However, Starbucks was willing to match my volunteered hours and provide funding to the organization upon the completion of my assignment. Initially, a friend that lived in California at the time asked a few people to join her while she volunteered in Texas for Hurricane Harvey victims. We wanted to actually volunteer when the hurricane hit; but, unfortunately, we could not. Timing is everything, though.

So, in March of 2018, AHAH reached out to see if I was still interested in volunteering. They booked me a flight and provided lodging and food for the entire time I was there. I stayed in a community style, co-ed living quarters at a church with people of all ages and different backgrounds. This experience reminded me of camp when I was a child. There were 10 bunk beds in each room, and our mornings started really early. I was praying that I didn't sleep in a room with someone who snored. And guess what. I did. He was a 73-year-old Canadian guy, sweet as pie but a very loud snorer. He was my bunkmate. I slept with headphones in my ears for an entire week and a half until we moved to our new location.

New volunteers rolled in every day and every week. I was able to meet a lot of people from all over the world. That was the most exciting part because I love people and diversity. During my volunteering experience, I learned how to muck and gut houses, how to get rid of mold and to sanitize walls. I learned how to measure wall spaces and how to put a wall up. That was super cool. And I did basic household fixers. I basically learned a new trade for free. You guys know I love learning, and I love free. If my experience sparked your interest, go to the website and learn how you can volunteer as well at www.allhandsandhearts.org.

Brian came home!

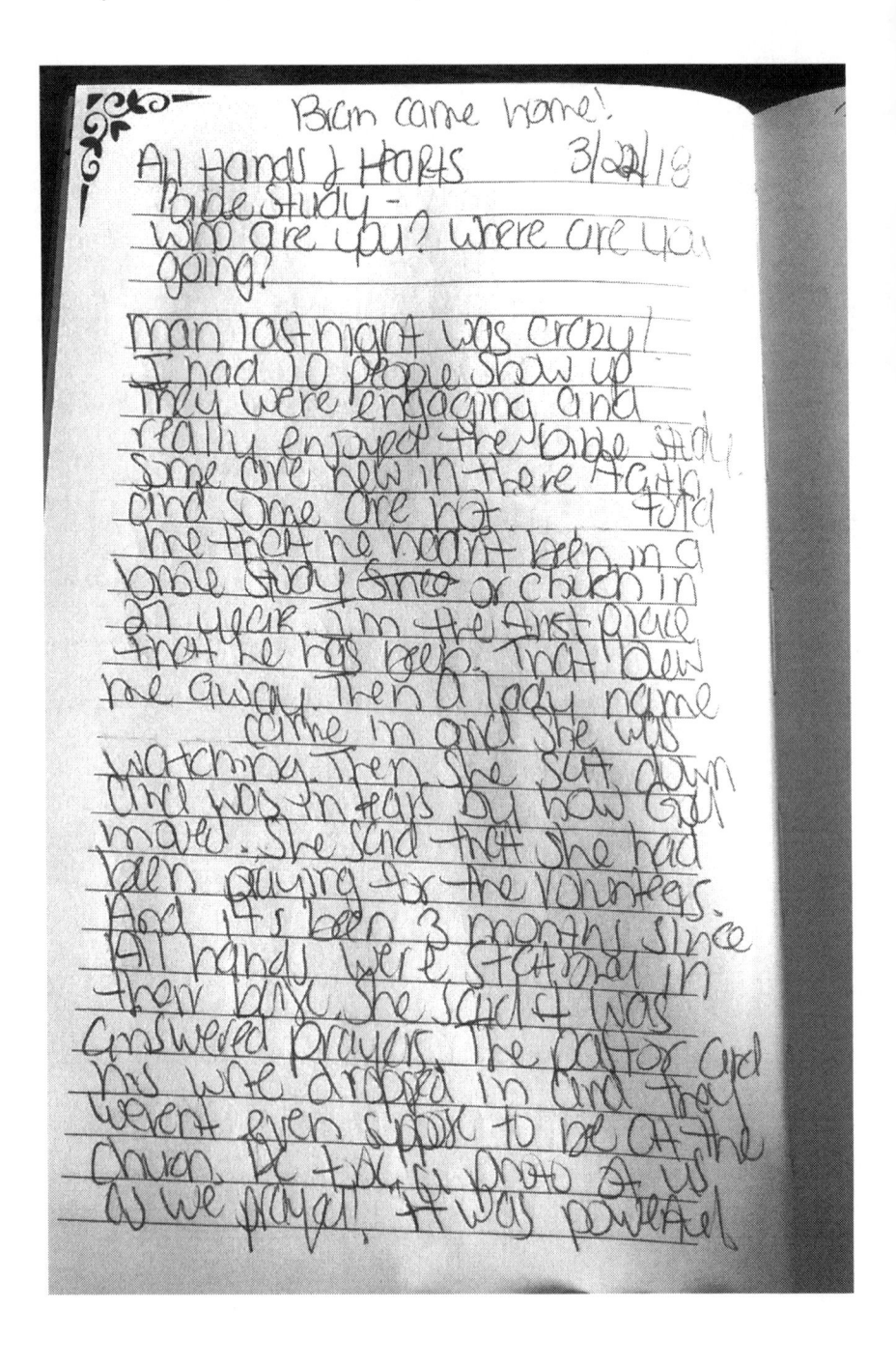

All Hands & Hearts   3/22/18
Bible Study -
Who are you? Where are you going?

Man last night was crazy! I had 10 people show up. They were engaging and really enjoyed the bible study. Some are new in their faith and some are not. [someone] told me that he hadn't been in a bible study since or church in a year. I'm the first place that he has been. That blew me away. Then a lady name ___ came in and she was watching. Then she sat down and was in tears by how God moved. She said that she had been praying for the volunteers. And it's been 3 months since All Hands were staying in their bunk. She said it was answered prayers. The pastor and his wife dropped in and they weren't even suppose to be at the church. He took a photo of us as we prayed. It was powerful.

March 13, 2018   Day 1
Disaster Relief: Houston, TX
All Hands & Hearts

Today I arrived in Texas at the disaster relief base. I took a Lyft and it was $90! I only paid $10. I am so lucky. We'll see. I got a top bunk right by the door and the bathroom. Yes God! I met a lady named ___ who is 31, from Nashville, TN! She had a cool. I bought a pillow and a cute backpack. I didn't want to spend the money but I'm not called to act broke. My ___ invited me to a comedy show next week and it's $35. God will provide in Jesus name! We finna have a ball! I love you God! I think the best part about this trip is worshipping God in this sanctuary. I just needed this and I will. I don't

Chapter 17
I'm Going Going, Back Back, To Cali, Cali

Okay, guys, we are going to fast forward just a tad bit, if that's okay. There are some events that I'd rather leave out, and that's perfectly fine. You may hear about them later. Okay, as I was planning my 3rd annual "Walk By Faith" Conference, I told the Lord that I didn't want it to be challenging and hard like the previous ones. God had already revealed to me that I would host the conference in Los Angeles. I want y'all to know that I was planning this conference remotely from Chicago, as I have done with the previous "Walk By Faith" Conference, if you've read the first *Blind Faith* book.

So, with this process. I simply said, "God, show me my venue and show me who will donate the space." Literally, God showed me the space in a vision and whispered the young lady's name in my ear. I heard his voice crystal clear. I prayed about it and thanked God and reached out to the young lady the next day. She answered the phone so energetically and lively. I voiced my request to her; and she immediately said, "Of course, Angel. And I'll pay for the rental fee." I mean, you guys, it was so easy that I actually had to reflect on it all. I was shocked and appreciative for God's love. He favored me.

So, the planning was simple and easy. I had decided that I wanted to actually have performers and vendors at the conference. I reached out to a few people and told them that I wanted to include them in my event. And surprisingly enough, they were all on board. Y'all, I had people flying out from Texas and Chicago, not to mention the individuals that were coming near and far from the surrounding Greater Los Angeles area. Besides that, I had my photographer/videographer and dancer all set and ready to go. I was excited about gathering a host of interviews of each participant and creating a dope video to display for the next conference attendees.

I was able to secure two sponsors. One of my really good male friends who is in real estate donated the pretty white folding chairs for my guests. My really good friend Kay made the food and the pastries. I mean, guys, this was such an easy planning process. Everyone was genuinely committed to helping me, and for this I am forever grateful. I managed to secure four vendors and seven speakers, and they all felt led to donate their time.

On the day of the event, I had so many hands to help decorate that I had to delegate the tasks. And my friend who has helped me with every conference was my go-to person. I mean I left to go get dressed. And when I got back, everything was set so beautifully. I mean BEAUTIFUL. Words cannot express the gratitude that I felt for each person who helped me. The guests arrived, and they were pleased with the setup. To me, presentation, professionalism and customer service are the most important aspects of planning an event. I love to create lasting impressions and experiences. We even dedicated a secluded corner for our prayer room.

So, at my childhood church, my pastor, Rev. Meeks, always made sure that we had several prayer rooms at our conferences. They all possessed different themes, fragrances and decor. So, I asked my Jamaican girlfriend to set my prayer room at the "Walk By Faith" conference by cultivating and ushering in the presence of God with prayer, holy oil and candles. It was such a warm environment to be in. There were many that went into the prayer room alone, and some even went in together. It was just beautiful.

All the panelists did a great job with answering questions and being transparent. The vendors were very engaging with the attendees and making a nice amount of sales. My photographer/videographer photographed and filmed the person conducting interviews of each speaker, vendor and many of the guests. The conference was more than what I could ask for.

Well, guys, sorry; but I'm going to end the book right here until we meet again in other *Blind Faith* sequels, interviews or some other national platform where I can tell the story.

PRAYER OF SALVATION

Father, I ask You to soften my heart for the deeper things of You. I ask that You forgive me of all of my iniquities. Heal me from all my infirmities and cause Your grace to saturate my entire being. Lord, give me the faith to endure this new chapter of my life and allow me to trust and grow in You. I believe that JESUS died on the cross for my sins and rose on the third day. I pray that if there is any area of unbelief of who You are or what You are capable of, I ask that You always reassure me. I ask that You constantly remind me of why I said yes to Your will and to Your way. Give me strength, wisdom, discernment and activate the spiritual gifts that are lying dormant in me that You may be glorified in all that I do. Give me the power to overthrow the works of the enemy in my life and in my bloodline. In Jesus' name I pray, Amen.

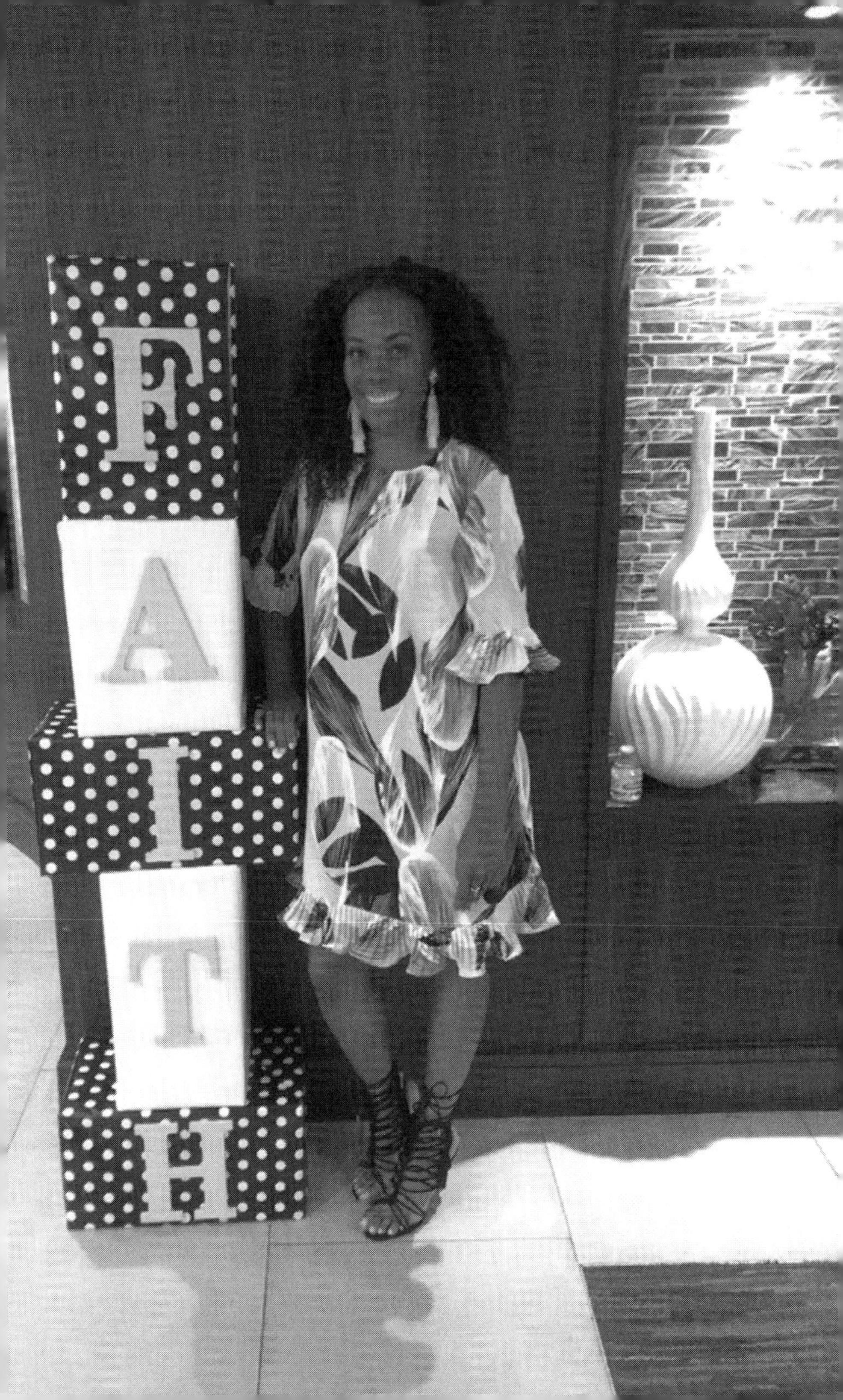
FAITH

EXTRA BONUS!

I had the wonderful opportunities to style Sage The Gemini and Faith Evans; I met Tiffani Haddish, Oprah Winfrey and went to a party at Eddie Murphy's estate in California.

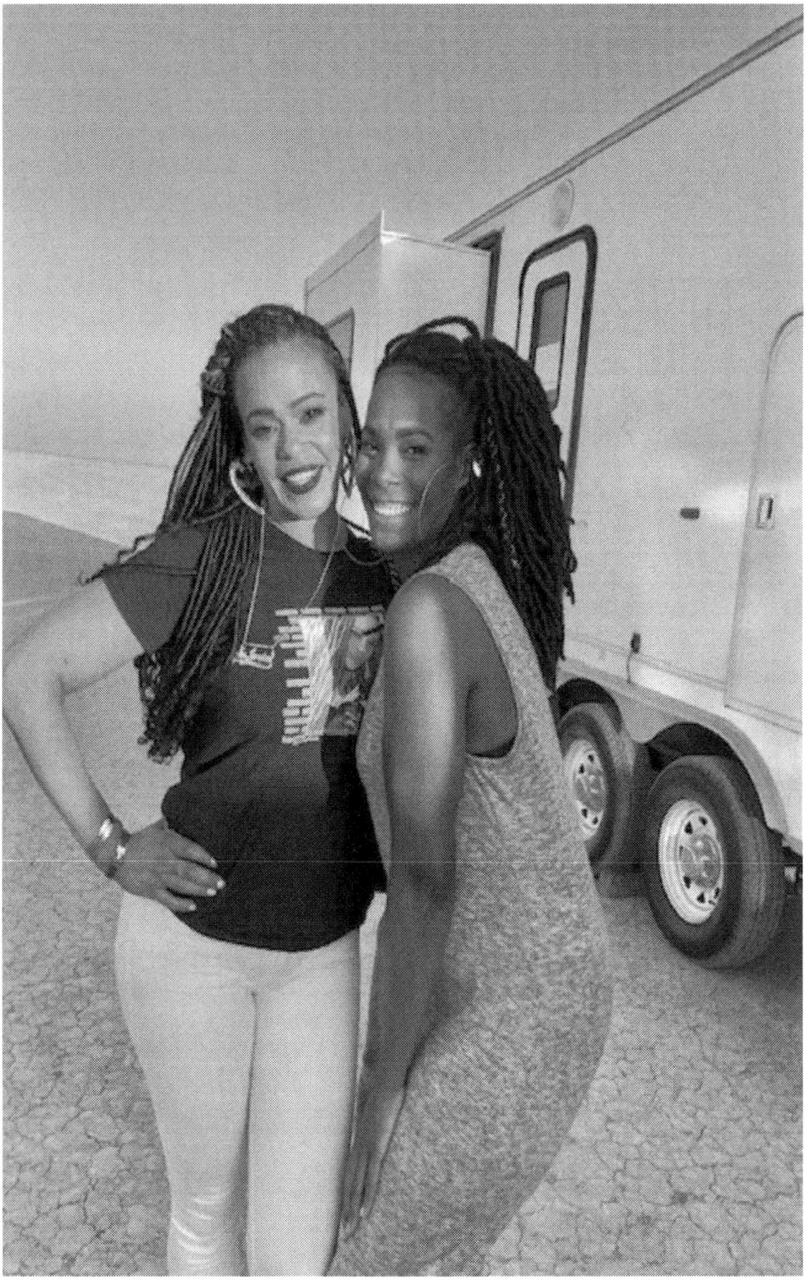

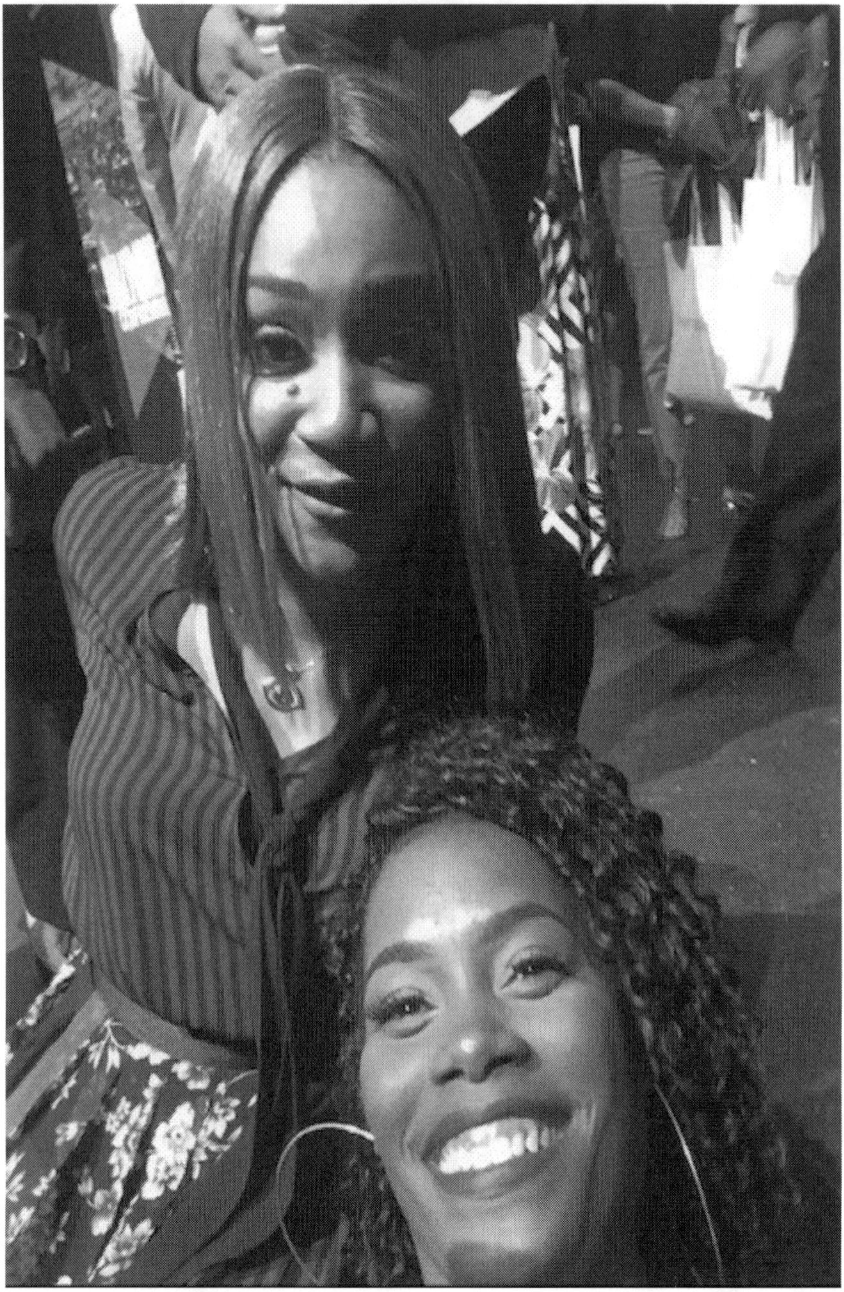

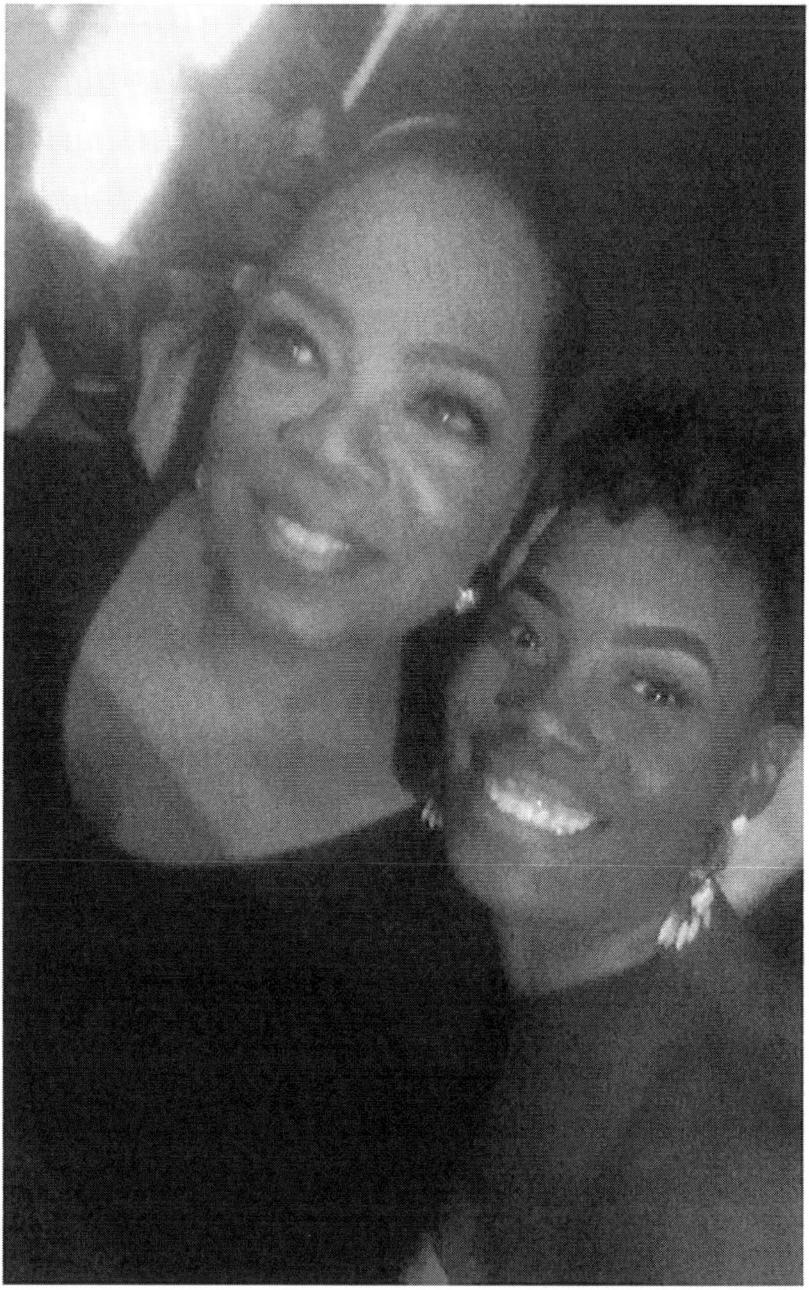

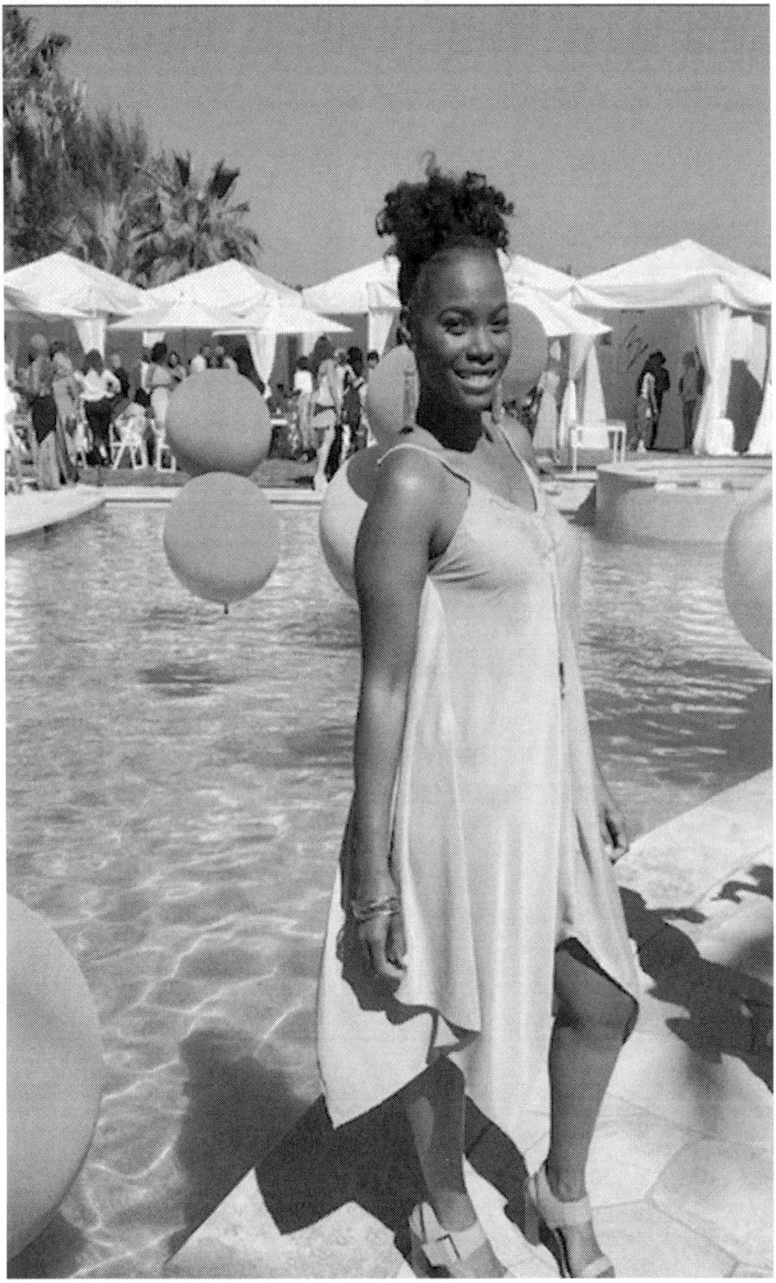

CONTACT INFORMATION:

Instagram:
@rawtalkstv
@lenorethelight
@thelenoreinc
@meiamourlenoir

Email:
Ministry & Speaking Inquiries – lenorethelight@gmail.com
Podcast Interviews - rawtalkstv@gmail.com
Coaching, Consulting & Events - thelenoreinc@gmail.com
Beauty & Apparel Inquiries - meiamourlenoir@gmail.com

Twitter:
Lenorethelight

TikTok:
Lenorethelight

Facebook Fan Page & FB Private Group
Lenore the Light & Lenorethelight Ministries

Youtube:
Rawtalkstv

Thank You For Reading
"THE DEEPER THINGS"

If you have been enlightened by the content of my book, I welcome you to write a review on my Amazon and/or Barnes & Noble author pages.

Made in the USA
Columbia, SC
20 July 2024

9611c08d-5c6a-4391-b012-039784111e3fR01